POCKET

SINGAPORE

TOP SIGHTS · LOCAL EXPERIENCES

D1216285

RIA DE JONG

Contents

Plan Your Trip 4

Performer at Chingay festival (p24)
SAM'S STUDIO/SHUTTERSTOCK ©

Explore Singapore 33

Worth a Trip

Survival Guide 177

Special Features

Welcome to Singapore

Smart, sharp and just a little sexy, Singapore is Southeast Asia's unexpected 'it kid', subverting staid stereotypes with ambitious architecture, dynamic museums, celebrity chefs and hip boutiques. Spike it with smoky temples, gut-rumble-inducing food markets and pockets of steamy jungle, and you'll find that Asia's former wallflower is a much more intriguing bloom than you ever gave it credit for.

Top Sights

Asian Civilisations Museum
Magnificent collection of pan-Asian treasures. **p36**

Gardens by the Bay

Singapore's high-tech futuristic garden. **p38**

National Gallery Singapore

World's leading collection of Southeast Asian art. **p40**

Singapore Zoo

A world-class tropical wonderland. **p96**

Night Safari

An exciting nocturnal adventure. **p98**

Singapore Botanic Gardens

Spectacular gardens. **p102**

Chinatown Heritage Centre
Step into the past. **p138**

Universal Studios
The city's biggest, busiest amusement park. **p128**

Southern Ridges
Singapore's most picturesque jungle trek. **p116**

Eating

Singaporeans are obsessed with makan (food), whether it's talking incessantly about their last meal to feverishly posting about it online. From eye-wateringly priced cutting-edge fine dining to dirt-cheap mouth-watering hawker fare, Singapore's cultural diversity has created one of the world's most varied culinary landscapes.

Hawker Grub

Hawker centres are usually standalone, open-air (or at least open-sided) structures with a raucous vibe and rows upon rows of food stalls peddling any number of local cuisines.

Often found in malls, food courts are basically air-conditioned hawker centres with marginally higher prices, while coffeeshops, also called *kopitiams*, are open-shopfront cafes, usually with a handful of stalls.

Wherever you are just dive in and get ordering (p149). Local wisdom suggests stalls with the longest queues are well worth the wait.

The Next Generation

As the older generation of hawkers barrel towards retirement, a new breed of innovative hawkers are taking up the challenge of dishing out great meals on the cheap. You'll find everything from Japanese ramen and Mexican street food, both with Singaporean twists, to old-school British fare and flavour-hit traditional sock-brewed *kopi* (coffee).

Fancy Fare

Singapore's restaurant scene is booming. From the ever-growing list of local and international celebrity-chef nosheries to a new breed of midrange eateries, delivering sharp, produce-driven menus in more relaxed settings, the options are endless. Clusters of big-hitters have transformed the areas around Chinatown's Amoy St and Keong Saik Rd into dining 'it' spots.

Best New-Gen Hawkers

Timbre+ A hawker hub with food trucks, craft suds and live tunes. (p122)

A Noodle Story Ramen with a Singaporean twist in Chinatown. (p147)

Coffee Break Singapore *kopi* meets hipster flavours at this Chinatown drink stall. (p141)

Best Hawker Eats

Maxwell Food Centre Chinatown's most tourist-friendly hawker centre. (p148)

Chinatown Complex The hard-core hawker experience. (p148)

Lau Pa Sat Worth a visit for its magnificent wrought-iron architecture alone. (pictured; p150)

Takashimaya Food Village A fabulous basement food hall on Orchard Rd. (p90)

Ya Kun Kaya Toast Historic hang-out serving Singapore's best runny eggs and *kaya* (coconut jam) toast. (p150)

Best Fusion & Western

Neon Pigeon Japanese iza-kaya share plates in Keong Saik. (p149)

Cheek by Jowl Beautifully crafted seasonal Australian fare. (p148)

Super Loco Customs House Mexican street food with a killer Marina Bay Sands view. (p52)

Butcher Boy Wow-oh-wow Asian-inspired creations for meat lovers. (p148)

Best Celeb-Chef Hot Spots

National Kitchen by Violet Oon Much-loved Peranakan favourites from the Julia Childs of Singapore. (p51)

Odette Modern French from Gallic superstar Julien Royer. (p51)

Iggy's Orchard Rd's most desirable culinary address helmed by Aitor Jeronimo Orive. (p87)

Burnt Ends Extraordinary barbecued meats from Australian expat Dave Pynt. (p147)

Waku Ghin Refined Japanese by acclaimed chef Tetsuya Wakuda. (p52)

Drinking & Nightlife

From speakeasy cocktail bars to boutique beer stalls to artisan coffee roasters, Singapore is discovering the finer points of drinking. The clubbing scene is no less competent, with newcomers including a futuristic club in the clouds, a basement hot spot fit for the streets of Tokyo, and a techno refuge in Boat Quay.

Cut-Price Drinks

Singapore is an expensive city to drink in. A beer at most city bars will set you back between S$10 and S$18, with cocktails commonly ringing in between S$20 and S$30. That said, many bars offer decent happy-hour deals, typically stretching from around 5pm to 8pm, sometimes starting earlier and finishing later. Those who don't mind plastic tables can always swill S$7 bottles of Tiger at the local hawker centre.

Kopi Culture

Single-origin beans and siphon brews may be all the rage among local hipsters, but Singapore's old-school *kopitiams* (coffeeshops) deliver the real local deal. Before heading in, it's a good idea to learn the lingo. *Kopi* means coffee with condensed milk, *kopi-o* is black coffee with sugar, while *kopi-c* gets you coffee with evaporated milk and sugar. If you need some cooling down, opt for a *kopi-peng* (iced coffee). Replace the word *kopi* with *teh* and

you have the same variation for tea. One local tea concoction worth sipping is *teh tarik* – literally 'pulled tea' – a sweet spiced Indian tea.

Best Wine Bars

Ginett Buzzing bar pouring possibly the cheapest glass of French plonk in town. (p77)

Que Pasa Classy little wine bar with an Iberian vibe in heritage Emerald Hill Rd. (p92)

Best Cocktails

Tippling Club Boundary-pushing libations from the bar that raised the bar. (pictured; p153)

BOAZ ROTTEM/ALAMY ©

28 HongKong Street
Passionate mixologists turning grog into greatness. (p54)

Native Surprising ingredients and clever twists in trendy Amoy St. (p153)

Manhattan Long-forgotten cocktails are given a new lease on life in this Orchard Rd heavyweight. (p91)

Best Clubs

Zouk A multivenue classic west of Robertson Quay. (p55)

Headquarters by the Council Thumping techno and house beats in this Boat Quay shophouse. (p56)

Taboo Hot bods and themed nights at Singapore's classic gay club. (p154)

Best Beers

Level 33 The world's highest craft brewery with a bird's-eye view of Marina Bay below. (p56)

Smith Street Taps A rotating cast of craft suds in a Chinatown hawker centre. (p154)

Druggists Twenty-three taps pouring craft brews in trendy Jalan Besar. (p74)

Best Coffee

Chye Seng Huat Hardware Superlative espresso, filter coffee, on-site roasting and classes. (p74)

Nylon Coffee Roasters A small, mighty espresso bar and roaster in Everton Park. (p152)

Coffee Break Singapore *kopi* meets hipster flavours in this Amoy St hawker stall. (p141)

The Singapore Sling

Granted, it tastes like cough syrup, but there's no denying the celebrity status of Singapore's most famous drink. Created by Raffles Hotel (p47) barman Ngiam Tong Boon, the Singapore sling first hit the bar in 1915. The recipe, once a tightly held secret, has long been out and now many Singapore bars peddle a modern (read: more palatable) twist on the original.

Shopping

While its shopping scene might not match the edge of Hong Kong's or Bangkok's, Singapore is no retail slouch. Look beyond the malls and you'll find everything from sharply curated local boutiques to vintage map peddlers and clued-in contemporary galleries.

Retail Road Map

While mall-heavy Orchard Rd is Singapore's retail queen, it's only one of several retail hubs. For electronics, hit tech mall Sim Lim Square. Good places for antiques include Tanglin Shopping Centre, Dempsey Hill and Chinatown. For fabrics and textiles, scour Little India and Kampong Glam; the latter is also known for perfume traders and indie-cool Haji Lane. For independent fashion, design and books, explore Tiong Bahru.

Bagging a Bargain

While Singapore is no longer a cut-price electronics nirvana, it can offer savings. Know the price of things beforehand, then browse and compare. Ask vendors what they can do to sweeten the deal; at the very least, they should be able to throw in a camera case or memory cards. Sim Lim Square mall is known for its range and negotiable prices, though it's also known for taking the uninitiated for a ride, not to mention for

occasionally selling 'new' equipment that isn't quite new: a quick internet search will bring up blacklisted businesses. The best deals are on computers and cameras, with prices often 20% lower than major stores.

Best for Design

Kapok Innovative threads and lifestyle objects at the National Design Centre. (p59)

Supermama Contemporary designer pieces with a Singaporean theme. (p79)

Bynd Artisan Handmade journals, leather travel accessories and jewellery. (p111)

SAM'S STUDIO/SHUTTERSTOCK ©

Best for Tech

Sim Lim Square Six levels of laptops, cameras and more at Singapore's biggest tech mall. (p81)

Mustafa Centre No shortage of electronic gizmos, available 24 hours a day. (p80)

Best Souvenirs

Raffles Hotel Gift Shop Everything from vintage poster prints to tea and tomes. (p59)

Antiques of the Orient Beautiful old maps, prints and photos of Singapore and the region. (p93)

Naiise Design-literate Singaporean trinkets and homewares. (p173)

National Gallery Singapore The museum store stocks tasteful, design-savvy gifts, including specially commissioned pieces. (p40)

Best Luxury Malls

ION Orchard Mall A-list boutiques in Singapore's most impressive consumer temple. (p93)

Shoppes at Marina Bay Sands Bayside luxury – and the world's first floating Louis Vuitton store. (pictured; p59)

Paragon Polished brands and a dedicated children's floor in the heart of Orchard Rd. (p93)

Best Midrange Malls

ION Orchard Mall ION's lower levels are dedicated to midrange fashion and accessories. (p93)

VivoCity Accessible labels galore at Singapore's biggest mall, just across from Sentosa. (p125)

Best for Art & Antiques

Tanglin Shopping Centre Quality Asian antiques and art in a mall off Orchard Rd. (p93)

Shang Antique Evocative temple artefacts and vintage Asian knick-knacks in Dempsey Hill. (p112)

For Kids

Safe, respectable, reliable Singapore would make an admirable babysitter. From interactive museums to an island packed with theme-park thrills, young ones are rarely an afterthought. Hotels supply cots, most cafes provide highchairs and modern malls have family rooms. If you're after family time, the Little Red Dot has you covered.

Sentosa: Pleasure Island

While kid-friendly attractions are spread out across Singapore, you'll find the greatest concentration on the island of Sentosa. Here you'll find the LA-style Universal Studios theme park, plus a long list of supporting attractions, from the ambitious SEA Aquarium to zip-lining and fake waves. You'll need at least a full day to experience everything Sentosa has to offer, not to mention a well-stocked wallet, as most activities, rides and shows cost extra.

Discounts

Kids receive up to 50% discount at most tourist venues. Those aged six years and under enjoy free entry to many of Singapore's top museums, including the National Gallery Singapore, National Museum of Singapore and the Asian Civilisations Museum. Kids under 0.9m tall can ride the MRT for free. Full-time students with photo ID cards also enjoy discounts at many attractions.

Best Thrills

Universal Studios Hollywood-inspired rides, roller coasters and shows for the young and young-at-heart. (p128)

iFly Plummet a virtual 2746m without a plane in sight at this indoor sky-diving centre. (p132)

Wave House Surf serious waves without ever leaving the pool on Sentosa. (p133)

Pinnacle@Duxton Affordable, family-friendly skypark with breathtaking city views and space to run around. (p146)

Best Museums

National Museum of Singapore An evocative exploration of Singaporean history and culture, with audiovisual displays, artefacts and child-friendly signs. (p46)

PUMPZA/SHUTTERSTOCK ©

ArtScience Museum
World-class art and science exhibitions with interactive kids' programs. (p48)

Lee Kong Chian Natural History Museum Engaging exhibits, complete with giant dinosaurs and fantastical displays of exotic beasts from both land and sea. (p120)

MINT Museum of Toys An impressive, Technicolor collection of over 50,000 rare, collectable toys. (p48)

Outdoor Adventures

Gardens by the Bay Space-age bio-domes, crazy Super-trees, bird's-eye Skyway and a 1-hectare Children's Garden, complete with wet play zones. (p38)

Southern Ridges Complete with dedicated children's playground, a treetop walk and the occasional monkey sighting. (p116)

Pulau Ubin Hop on a bike and cycle through forest and past colourful shacks on this tranquil, relatively flat, stuck-in-time island. (p174)

Singapore Ducktours Embarrassingly fun tours on a brightly coloured amphibious former military vehicle. (p49)

Best Animal Watching

Singapore Zoo Breakfast with orang-utans at one of the world's role-model zoological gardens. (p96)

Night Safari Spend the evening with leopards, lions and Himalayan blue sheep at this atmospheric wildlife oasis. (p98)

SEA Aquarium A spectacular, comprehensive aquarium. (pictured; p131)

Strolling Around

Singapore is a dream for families using strollers. Footpaths are well maintained, accessing public transport is a breeze (wheel straight onto trains and buses) and large attractions often have strollers for hire.

History & Culture

Singapore's history and culture is show-cased in its numerous and extremely well-curated museums and sights. You'll find the biggest and the best in the Colonial District, where collections dive into the area's history, culture and art. Beyond them are unexpected treasures, from reconstructed Chinatown slums to haunting wartime memorials.

WWII Sites

Singapore's WWII experience was a watershed period in its history. It's covered in depth in many museums, including the National Museum of Singapore and Former Ford Factory. It's also commemorated at several wartime sites, including a British fort on Sentosa, the battleground of Bukit Chandu (Opium Hill) and a former bunker in Fort Canning Park. Not surprisingly, the trauma of occupation and Singapore's tetchy postwar relations with its larger neighbours have fuelled its obsession with security today.

Best Peranakan Pickings

Peranakan Museum Delve into the Peranakan world of marriage, storytelling, fashion, feasting and mourning in atmospheric, multimedia galleries. (p46)

Baba House Step into the private world of a wealthy Peranakan family, c 1928, at one of Singapore's most beautiful historic homes. (p144)

Katong Antique House A cluttered collection of historical objects and stories from one of Singapore's leading Peranakan historians. (p165)

Best for War History

Fort Siloso Slip into subterranean tunnels at this ill-fated defence fort on Sentosa Island. (p131)

Reflections at Bukit Chandu A gripping retelling of the Japanese invasion atop former battlefield Opium Hill. (p117)

Battlebox This haunting underground complex documents the swift fall of Singapore. (p46)

Best for Art & Handicrafts

National Gallery Singapore Singapore's biggest cultural asset showcases 19th- and 20th-century regional art. (p40)

EQROY/SHUTTERSTOCK ©

Asian Civilisations Museum A pan-Asian treasure trove of decorative arts, religious artefacts, art and textiles. (p36)

Gillman Barracks A rambling artillery of private galleries exhibiting modern and contemporary art. (p120)

Best for Old Singapore

National Museum of Singapore Explore centuries of Singaporean history, from exiled Sumatran princes to independence. (p46)

Chinatown Heritage Centre Relive the gritty, chaotic and overcrowded Chinatown of yesteryear. (p138)

Images of Singapore Live A child-friendly interactive panorama spanning six centuries of local history. (p131)

Indian Heritage Centre A state-of-the-art museum showcasing the origins and heritage of Singapore's Indian community. (p66)

Best Temples, Mosques & Churches

Thian Hock Keng Temple Stands proud with its stone lions and elaborately carved beams. (p144)

Sultan Mosque The golden-domed hub that holds Kampong Glam together. (p66)

Sri Veeramakaliamman Temple Little India's most colourful, and stunning Hindu temple. (pictured; p67)

St Andrew's Cathedral Whitewashed wedding-cake elegance of Singapore's most famous church. (p43)

Former Ford Factory

The former Ford Motors assembly plant is best remembered as the place where the British surrendered Singapore to the Japanese on 15 February 1942. It's now home to an exhibition that charts Singapore's descent into war, the three dark years of Japanese occupation and Singapore's recovery and path to independence.

Entertainment

Singapore's nightlife calendar is generally booked solid. There's live music, theatre and adrenalin-pumping activities year-round, but at certain times of the year the city explodes into a flurry of car racing, cultural festivals and hot-ticket music events. When that all gets too much, Singapore's spas are waiting in the wings.

Film

Singaporeans love to watch movies and, at around S$12.50 per ticket, it's great value. Multiplex cinemas abound with many located in larger malls. The annual Singapore International Film Festival screens independent and art-house films. Singapore's cinemas are chilly, so wear something warm.

Live Music

An enthusiastic local music scene thrives (to a point). Esplanade – Theatres on the Bay hosts regular free performances and is home to the Singapore Symphony Orchestra. Top-tier international talent is showcased at both the Singapore International Jazz Festival and indie favourite St Jerome's Laneway Festival.

Booking Events

Check what's on and buy tickets at www.sistic.com.sg. Expect to pay from S$20 to S$70 for a ticket to a local theatre production, S$100 to S$300 for international music acts, and S$65 to S$200 for big-budget musicals. Gigs by local music acts are often free, though some places have a small cover charge.

Best for Live Music

BluJaz Café Consistently good jazz and blues in Kampong Glam. (p78)

Timbrè @ The Substation Local bands and singer-songwriters in the Colonial District. (p58)

Crazy Elephant Rock and blues in party-central Clarke Quay. (p58)

Esplanade – Theatres on the Bay Polished performances spanning classical to rock. (pictured; p49)

Timbre+ Live music at this New Age hawker centre. (p122)

TERENCE WONG/SHUTTERSTOCK ©

Best for Theatre

Singapore Repertory Theatre A world-class repertoire that includes seasonal Shakespeare at Fort Canning Park. (p58)

Wild Rice Reinterpreted classics, new works and striking sets. (p79)

TheatreWorks New commissions and international collaborations. (p58)

Necessary Stage Locally flavoured, thought-provoking theatre. (p171)

Best for Chinese Performance

Chinese Theatre Circle Chinese opera, talks, performances and meals in Chinatown. (p155)

Singapore Chinese Orchestra Classical Chinese concerts performed with traditional instruments. (p155)

Best Spectator Sports

Singapore Formula One Grand Prix The F1 night race screams around Marina Bay in late September. (p24)

Rugby Sevens Singapore joined the list of host countries for the World Rugby Cup series in 2016.

Best for Classic & Indie Films

Screening Room Cult and classic flicks in an intimate suite in Chinatown. (p154)

Rex Cinemas Bollywood hits on the edge of Little India. (p78)

Worth a Trip

Though not quite as manic as the Hong Kong races, a trip to **Singapore Turf Club** (☎6879 1008; www.turfclub.com.sg; 1 Turf Club Ave; from S$6; Ⓜ Kranji) is a hugely popular day out. Race times vary but usually run on Friday evenings and Sunday afternoons. A dress code is enforced (see website details) and entry is over 18s only, so bring photo ID. Entry to the Owners' Lounge is S$30.

Tours

Although Singapore is one of the world's easiest cities for self-navigation, guided tours can open up the city and its history in unexpected ways. Tours and cruises span everything from fun, family-friendly overviews to specialised themed adventures.

Touring 101

Singapore is hot and humid so, when going on a tour, make sure you dress in clothes that are lightweight, breathable and comfortable.

If you're headed outdoors a hat, sunscreen, water and insect repellent are a must, and an umbrella is handy for tropical downpours. Food tours are a gastronomic delight and you should arrive with a rumbling tummy; an expandable waistband is optional but suggested.

Best Themed Tours

Betel Box: The Real Singapore Tours Led by Tony Tan and the team at the Betel Box hostel. (p167)

Jane's SG Tours Insightful tours offering a unique look into Singapore's history, architecture, religions, botany and culture. (p88)

Battlebox Head underground to discover the tunnels and rooms of this historic WWII bunker. (p46)

Bukit Brown Tour (www. facebook.com/groups/ bukitbrown) Fascinating walking tours through Bukit Brown, one of Singapore's most historic, wild and beautiful cemeteries.

Best Hop-On, Hop-Off Tours

Singapore 7 Sightseeing (www.singapore7.com) Passing major tourist areas on several routes, this double-decker, open-top tourist bus allows you to hop on and off as many times as you like.

SIA Hop-On (www.siahop on.com) Traversing the main tourist arteries every 15 to 60 minutes daily, Singapore Airlines' tourist bus runs four different lines.

Best Neighbourhood Tours

Original Singapore Walks (www.singaporewalks.com) Knowledgable on-foot

SAM'S STUDIO/SHUTTERSTOCK ©

excursions through Chinatown, Little India, Kampong Glam, the Colonial District, Boat Quay, Haw Par Villa and war-related sites. Most tours last from 2½ to three hours and do not require a booking; check the website for meeting times and places.

Chinatown Trishaw Night Tour (www.viator.com) An atmospheric four-hour tour of Chinatown including dinner, on-foot exploration, a trishaw ride and a bumboat river cruise along the Sing-apore River. Hotel pick-ups and drop-offs are provided.

Trishaw Uncle Hop on a trishaw for an old-fashioned ride through Bugis and Little India. The 45-minute tour also takes in the Singapore River.

You'll find the trishaw terminal on Queen St, between the Fu Lu Shou Complex and the Albert Centre Market and Food Centre. (p70)

Best River Tours

Singapore River Cruise
Relaxing, 40-minute bumboat cruises that ply the stretch between the Quays and Marina Bay with spectacular views of the city. (p49)

Singapore Ducktours
Embarrassingly fun tours on a brightly coloured amphibious former military vehicle. (pictured; p49)

Worth a Trip

Visits to the **Tiger Brewery** (☎ 6860 3005; www.tigerbrewerytour.com.sg; 459 Jln Ahmad Ibrahim; adult/child S$18/12; ⏱ 1-6.30pm Tue-Sun; Ⓟ; Ⓜ Tuas West Rd) are divided into two parts: a 45-minute tour of the place followed by 45 minutes of free beer tasting in the wood-and-leather Tiger Tavern. Tours run on the hour from 1pm to 5pm and must be booked in advance. Under 18s will only be admitted with an adult and are not allowed alcoholic drinks.

Festivals

Singapore is the ultimate melting pot. With four official languages, it's a place where mosques sidle up to temples, European chefs experiment with Chinese spices, and local English is peppered with Hokkien, Tamil and Malay. This rich, vibrant multicultural heritage is celebrated year-round through a plethora of diverse festivals.

SAM'S STUDIO/SHUTTERSTOCK ©

Best Music Festivals

St Jerome's Laneway Festival (January; http://singapore.lanewayfestival.com) Uberhip one-day indie music fest.

Singapore International Jazz Festival (April; www.sing-jazz.com) Three-day showcase of jazz talent.

ZoukOut (December; www.zoukout.com) Singapore's biggest outdoor dance party, held over two nights on Sentosa with A-list international DJs.

Best Chinese Festivals

Chinese New Year (February) Dragon dances, fireworks, food and spectacular street decorations.

Mid-Autumn Festival (August/September) Lanterns light up Chinatown as revellers nibble on mooncakes. Held on the full moon of the 8th lunar month.

Best Hindu Festivals

Thaipusam (February) Kavadis (heavy metal frames) pierce parading devotees.

Diwali (October/November) Little India glows for the 'Festival of Lights'.

Thimithi (October/November) Hindus walk over white-hot coals at Sri Mariamman Temple.

Best for Foodies

Singapore Food Festival (July; www.yoursingapore.com) Two weeks of tastings, special dinners and food-themed tours.

World Gourmet Summit (March/April; www.worldgourmetsummit.com) Four weeks of top chefs, workshops and lavish dinners.

Best Unique Singapore Festivals

Chingay (February; www.chingay.org.sg) Singapore's biggest street party, held on the 22nd day after Chinese New Year.

Singapore National Day (9 August) Extravagant processions and fireworks. Buy tickets in advance.

Singapore Formula One Grand Prix (September; www.singaporegp.sg) Spectacular after-dark F1 racing.

Views & Vistas

Admit it: posting hot travel shots online to torture friends is fun – and Singapore makes the perfect partner in crime. From dramatic skyline panoramas to close-up shots of brightly coloured shutters, food and lurid tropical flora, the city is ridiculously photogenic. So take aim, shoot and expect no shortage of gratifying Likes.

BULE SKY STUDIO/SHUTTERSTOCK ©

Best Skyline Vistas

Smoke & Mirrors Point-blank views of the Padang and Marina Bay skyline from this stylish rooftop bar at the National Gallery of Singapore. (p54)

ION Sky Observation deck on level 56 of the ION Orchard Mall. (p93)

CÉ LA VI SkyBar Cocktails and gobsmacking city vistas from this bar perched atop Marina Bay Sands. (p55)

1-Altitude Rooftop Gallery & Bar 360-degree island views await at the world's highest alfresco bar, 282m above CBD traffic. (p56)

Best for Architecture Buffs

Gardens by the Bay High-tech trees, epic bio-domes, a soaring indoor waterfall and striking sculptures. (p38)

National Gallery Singapore A breathtaking synergy of colonial architecture and innovative contemporary design. (p40)

Chinatown Ornate heritage shophouses and smoky temples with stories to tell. (p137)

Marina Bay Sands A three-tower sci-fi fantasy. (p46)

Emerald Hill Rd An evocative mix of lantern-lit shophouses and elegant, early 20th-century residences. (p86)

Best Is-This-Really Singapore?

Little India Colouring-book facades, shrines and garland stalls, mini mountains of spice and dazzling saris. (p61)

Kampong Glam An *Arabian Nights* fantasy of late-night cafes, intricate Persian rugs and a whimsical, golden-domed mosque. (p61)

Pulau Ubin Tin-roof shacks, free-roaming farm animals and rambling jungle wilderness channel a Singapore long since lost. (p174)

Geylang Road An after-dark world of neon-lit karaoke bars, *kopitiams* (coffeeshops) and seedy side streets with temples and sex workers. (p160)

Four Perfect Days

Day 1

Take a morning stroll on the **Quays** (p53) for a stunning panorama of brazen skyscrapers and refined colonial buildings, before exploring the remarkable **Asian Civilisations Museum** (p36). Sample some Peranakan perfection at **National Kitchen by Violet Oon** (p51), before seeing the world-class collection of Southeast Asian art at the **National Gallery Singapore** (p40).

In the afternoon discover the temples of **Chinatown** (p137). **Sri Mariamman Temple** (p146) and **Buddha Tooth Relic Temple** (pictured; p144) offer glimpses into neighbourhood life. Then have a pre-dinner tipple on Club St and an early dinner of iconic chilli crab at **Jumbo Seafood** (p51).

Complete your evening with a visit to the nocturnal **Night Safari** (p98).

Day 2

Little India (p61) will erase every preconceived notion of Singapore as a sterile, OCD metropolis. Take in the colours and chanting of **Sri Veeramakaliamman Temple** (p67) before visiting the **Indian Heritage Centre** (p66), to learn the area's fascinating backstory. For lunch turn up the heat at curry house **Lagnaa Barefoot Dining** (p71).

Beat the afternoon heat by heading to the air-conditioned **ION Orchard Mall** (pictured; p83) before enjoying a happy-hour tipple on heritage beauty **Emerald Hill Road** (p86).

When your tummy starts to rumble head to **Satay by the Bay** (p53) and then go exploring the futuristic **Gardens by the Bay** (p38) – don't miss the Supertrees light show (7.45pm and 8.45pm).

Day 3

Wake up early to join the orang-utans for **Jungle Breakfast with Wildlife** (p97) at the world-class **Singapore Zoo** (p96). Note feeding times, as the animals are more active then and you have the opportunity to get up-close and personal.

After all that wildlife, it's time for some pure, unadulterated fun on **Sentosa Island** (pictured; p127). Tackle rides at movie theme park **Universal Studios** (p128), ride some artificial waves at **Wave House** (p133) or book an indoor skydive at **iFly** (p132).

Finally slow down the pace with evening drinks and dinner on a palm-fringed Sentosa beach. Options include family-friendly **Coastes** (p135) or the more secluded **Tanjong Beach Club** (p134).

Day 4

For a taste of 1950s Singapore, indulge in a local breakfast of *kaya* (coconut jam) toast, runny eggs and strong *kopi* (coffee) at **Chin Mee Chin Confectionery** (p169). Then wander the shophouse-lined streets of **Joo Chiat (Katong)** (p163). Don't miss the pastel beauties on **Koon Seng Road** (p165), before slurping a bowl of cult-status laksa from **328 Katong Laksa** (p168).

Work off lunch by renting a bicycle and cycling the peaceful **East Coast Park** (p167), watching the numerous ships cruising the Strait of Singapore.

In the evening, swap tranquillity for neon-lit **Geylang** (p160), a red-light district juxtaposed with temples, mosques and some of the best food in Singapore. End your night at rooftop bar **Smoke & Mirrors** (p54), where you'll enjoy commanding city views.

Need to Know

For detailed information, see Survival Guide (p177)

Currency
Singapore dollar (S$)

Language
English, Mandarin, Bahasa Malaysia, Tamil

Visas
Citizens of most countries are granted 90-day entry on arrival.

Money
ATMs and money-changers are widely available. Credit cards are widely accepted.

Mobile Phones
Numbers start with 9 or 8. Buy tourist SIM cards (around S$15) from post offices, convenience stores and telco stores – by law you must show your passport.

Time
Singapore is (GMT/UTC plus eight hours

Tipping
Generally not customary, and prohibited at Changi Airport.

Daily Budget

Budget: Less than S$200
Dorm bed: S$25–45

Meals at hawker centres and food courts: around S$6

One-hour foot reflexology at People's Park Complex: S$25

Ticket to a major museum: S$6–20

Midrange: S$200–400
Double room in midrange hotel: S$150–300

Singapore Ducktour: S$43

Two-course dinner with wine: S$80

Cocktail at a decent bar: S$20–28

Top End: More than S$400
Four- or five-star double room: S$350–800

Massage at Remède Spa: S$105

Degustation in top restaurant: S$300-plus

Theatre ticket: S$150

Advance Planning

Two months before Book big-ticket events such as the Formula One race. Reserve a table at a hot top-end restaurant.

One month before Book a bed if you're planning to stay in a dorm over the weekend.

One week before Look for last-minute deals on Singapore accommodation and check for any events or festivals. Book a posh hotel brunch or high tea.

Arriving in Singapore

✈ Changi Airport

MRT trains run into town from the airport from 5.30am to 11.18pm; public buses run from 6am to midnight. Both the train and bus trips cost from S$1.69. The airport shuttle bus (adult/child S$9/6) runs 24 hours a day. A taxi into the city will cost anywhere from S$20 to S$40, and up to 50% more between midnight and 6am, plus airport surcharges. A four-seater limousine taxi is S$55, plus a S$15 surcharge per additional stop.

⚓ HarbourFront Cruise Ferry Terminal

MRT trains into town cost from S$1.07. A taxi will cost from S$8 to S$13, plus any surcharges.

🚆 Woodlands Train Checkpoint

Taxis into town cost from S$25 to S$30, plus any surcharges.

Getting Around

Ⓜ MRT

The local subway – the most convenient way to get around between 5.30am and midnight.

🚌 Bus

Go everywhere the trains do and more. Great for views. Run from 5am to 1am the following day, plus some later night buses from the city.

🚕 Taxi

These are fairly cheap if you're used to Sydney or London prices, though there are hefty surcharges during peak hours and from midnight to 6am. Flag one on the street or at a taxi stand. Good luck getting one on rainy days.

🚗 Grab

Singapore's answer to Uber, which it took over in 2018.

Singapore
Neighbourhoods

*Singapore Zoo &
Night Safari*
(12km)

West & Southwest Singapore (p115)

An urban getaway of jungle canopy walks, hilltop cocktails, historic war sites – an off-the-radar cultural gem.

Holland Village, Dempsey Hill & the Botanic Gardens (p101)

Latte-sipping expats, boutique antiques in converted colonial barracks and the luxurious sprawl of Singapore Botanic Gardens.

*Singapore
Botanic
Gardens* ◉

*Southern
Ridges*
◉

◉
*Universal
Studios*

Sentosa Island (p127)

Welcome to Fantasy Island, a 'think big' playground of theme parks, activities and shows, sunset beach bars and marina-side dining.

Orchard Road (p83)
Malls, malls, malls –
from the futuristic to
the downright retro,
this air-conditioned
thoroughfare is to retail
what Las Vegas' Strip is
to gambling.

**Joo Chiat (Katong)
(p163)**
Spiritual home of
Singapore's Peranakan
community, peppered
with multicoloured
shophouses, shrines and
some of the island's best
local food spots.

**Little India & Kampong
Glam (p61)**
The Singapore you
didn't think existed:
gritty, Technicolor
laneways bursting with
life, sheesha cafes and
independent boutiques.

National Gallery Singapore
Asian Civilisations Museum

Chinatown
Heritage
Centre

Gardens
by the
Bay

**Colonial District, the
Quays & Marina Bay
(p35)**
Dashing colonial
buildings mixed with
modern marvels, world-
class museums and
riverfront dining.

**Chinatown & the CBD
(p137)**
A mix of incense-heady
temples and sizzling
hawker centres, sky-
scrapers and shophouses
and jammed with trendy
restaurants and bars.

Explore
Singapore

Worth a Trip

Gardens by the Bay (p38) TAKASHI IMAGES/SHUTTERSTOCK ©

Explore

Colonial District, the Quays & Marina Bay

The former British administrative enclave is Singapore's showcase, home to a swath of grand colonial buildings, modern architectural marvels, and superlative museums and parks. The Singapore River connects the three quays, which bring a buzzing nocturnal life to the area.

The Short List

∘ **Asian Civilisations Museum (p36)** *Admiring Southeast Asia's finest collection of pan-Asian treasures.*

∘ **Gardens by the Bay (p38)** *Leaping into a sci-fi future at Singapore's spectacular botanic gardens.*

∘ **National Gallery Singapore (p40)** *Wandering the grand home of the world's largest public display of modern Southeast Asian art.*

∘ **Marina Bay Sands (p46)** *Pondering Singaporean ambition from the top of one of the world's greatest engineering feats.*

∘ **Peranakan Museum (p46)** *Exploring the colour-saturated culture of the Peranakans.*

Getting There & Around

Ⓜ The MRT is centred on City Hall, an interchange station that's also connected via underground malls towards the Esplanade, from where you can cut across to Marina Bay. Raffles Place (East–West Line) is the next stop for the Quays. The Bayfront MRT (Downtown Line) serves Marina Bay Sands, Gardens by the Bay and Fort Canning.

Neighbourhood Map on p44

Downtown Singapore TAPANUTH/SHUTTERSTOCK ©

Top Sight 📷
Asian Civilisations Museum

The remarkable Asian Civilisations Museum houses the region's most comprehensive collection of pan-Asian treasures. Over three levels, its beautifully curated galleries explore Singapore's heritage as a port city and the connections, history, cultures and religions of Southeast Asia, China, the Indian subcontinent and Islamic west Asia. These aspects are then further explored in the context of Asia and the rest of the world.

◎ MAP P44, D4

📞 6332 7798; 1 Empress Pl

www.acm.org.sg

adult/student/child under 6yr S$20/15/free, 7-9pm Fri half price

🕙 10am-7pm Sat-Thu, to 9pm Fri

Ⓜ Raffles Place, City Hall

Tang Shipwreck

Having sunk more than 1000 years ago, the Tang Shipwreck offers an insight into the history of trade throughout Asia in the 9th century. Laden with exquisite objects and over 60,000 Tang dynasty ceramics, its discovery was literally finding hidden treasure. The mesmerising sea of Changsha bowls surround a replica wooden plank boat, held together by coconut husk rope. Don't bother trying to see your reflection in the ornate bronze mirrors – their silvery alloy has been blackened from centuries underwater. One was even an antique before setting sail and is now over 2000 years old!

Trade Gallery

As people migrated around the region, so did their ideas, tastes and goods. The collection of porcelain is especially strong, covering the history of the different regions in which it was produced. Don't miss the intense blue-and-white Chinese and Middle Eastern ceramics. One for slightly different tastes is the brightly coloured boar's-head tureen and underdish – complete with open nostrils for the steam to escape, it must have made quite the spectacle on its owner's dinner table. It wasn't all about porcelain in the Tang dynasty era, though – the intricate silver tea set was made in China and is one of the few remaining still with its original box.

Ancient Religions Gallery

Ancient Indian religions also spread throughout Asia from the 3rd century BC, specifically Hinduism and Buddhism, and this gallery showcases the changes in religious images that occurred as the new was meshed with the old. Don't miss the terracotta head of a Bodhisattva, whose mane of hair, beard and headdress is incredibly detailed. This gallery is still a work in progress as the museum intends to delve further into the transformations of these religions and others in Asia.

★ Top Tips

o The 3rd-level galleries are only accessible from the stairs and the lift at the rear of the building.

o Mornings are the quietest time to visit to avoid crowds.

o If you enter via the River Entrance, make sure you exit out the main lobby doors to see the building's impressive facade.

✕ Take a Break

An outlet of the Privé (p92) chain can be found in the museum lobby, perfect for a spot of coffee with a nice view of the Singapore River.

Colonial District, the Quays & Marina Bay Asian Civilisations Museum

Top Sight 📷

Gardens by the Bay

Welcome to the botanic gardens of the future, a fantasy land of space-age bio-domes, high-tech Supertrees and whimsical sculptures. Costing S$1 billion and sprawling across 101 hectares of reclaimed land, Gardens by the Bay is more than a mind-clearing patch of green. This ambitious masterpiece of urban planning is as thrilling to architecture buffs as it is to nature lovers.

◉ MAP P44, H6

📲 6420 6848

www.gardensbythebay.
com.sg

18 Marina Gardens Dr

gardens free, conservatories adult/child under 13 yr S$28/15

The Conservatories

Housing 226,000 plants from 800 species, the Gardens' asymmetrical conservatories rise like giant paper nautilus shells beside Marina Bay. The Flower Dome replicates a dry, Mediterranean climate and includes ancient olive trees. It's also home to sophisticated restaurant Pollen, which sources ingredients from the Gardens. Cloud Forest Dome is a steamy affair, re-creating the tropical montane climate found at elevations between 1500m and 3000m. Its centrepiece is a 35m-high mountain complete with waterfall.

Supertrees & Sculptures

Sci-fi meets botany at the Supertrees, 18 steel-clad concrete structures adorned with over 162,900 plants. Actually massive exhausts for the Gardens' bio-mass steam turbines, they're used to generate electricity to cool the conservatories. For a sweeping view, walk across the 22m-high **OCBC Skyway**, (adult/child under 13 yr S$8/5) connecting six Supertrees at Supertree Grove, where tickets can be bought (cash only, last ticket sale 8pm). Each night at 7.45pm and 8.45pm, the Supertrees become the glowing protagonists of Garden Rhapsody, a light-and-sound spectacular. The most visually arresting of the Gardens' numerous artworks is Mark Quinn's colossal *Planet*. Created in 2008, the sculpture is a giant seven-month-old infant (modelled on Quinn's own son), fast asleep and seemingly floating above the ground.

Far East Organization Children's Garden

Little ones are wonderfully catered for at this interactive garden, specifically designed for kids up to 13 years old. Let them go wild on the obstacle-dotted Adventure Trail and suspension-bridge-linked Treehouses. Finally cool down at the Water Play Zone, complete with motion-sensing water effects and piped-in music.

★ Top Tips

o The nearest MRT station to the Gardens is Bayfront.

o Gardens by the Bay operates a handy, on-site **shuttle bus** (9am-9pm, 1st Mon of month from 12.30pm). Buy tickets on board (small denominations of cash only).

o The conservatories are open 5am-2am and the OCBC Skyway is open 9am-9pm.

✗ Take a Break

Fine dine in the Flower Dome at **Pollen** (6604 9988; www.pollen.com.sg; a la carte 2/3 courses S$88/98, set lunch 3/5 courses S$55/85, 6-course dinner tasting menu S$155; noon-2.30pm & 6-9.30pm Wed-Mon, Pollen Terrace cafe 9am-9pm Wed-Mon). The restaurant also hosts an excellent afternoon tea.

For a cheaper feed, opt for alfresco hawker centre Satay by the Bay (p53).

Top Sight 📷
National Gallery Singapore

*Ten years in the making, the S$530 million
National Gallery is a fitting home for what is one
of the world's most important surveys of colonial
and post-colonial Southeast Asian art. Housed
in the historic City Hall and Old Supreme Court
buildings, its 8000-plus collection of 19th-century
and modern Southeast Asian art fills two major
gallery spaces.*

◎ MAP P44, D3

📞 6271 7000

www.nationalgallery.sg

St Andrew's Rd

adult/child S$20/15

🕙 10am-7pm Sat-Thu, to
9pm Fri

P; M City Hall

The Buildings

Unified by a striking aluminium and glass canopy, Singapore's former City Hall (p43) and Old Supreme Court buildings are now joined to create the country's largest visual arts venue spanning a whopping 64,000 sq metres. Enter via the St Andrew's Rd door to get a real appreciation of how these colonial giants have been seamlessly connected. The two buildings have played pivotal roles in Singapore's journey; City Hall was where the Japanese surrendered to Singapore in 1945 and where Singapore's first prime minister, Lee Kuan Yew, was sworn in. Tours are held daily; don't miss the court holding cells, where many of Singapore's accused waited to hear their fates.

DBS Singapore Gallery

Titled 'Siapa Nama Kamu?' (Malay for 'What Is Your Name?'), this gallery showcases a comprehensive overview of Singaporean art from the 19th century to today. Don't miss Chua Mia Tee's *Portrait of Lee Boon Ngan* in Gallery Two; take note of how her collar sparkles. Also in this gallery, look out for the black-and-white woodblock prints; *Seascape* was a collaboration of six artists. Finally, have your mind bent by Matthew Ngui's *Walks Through a Chair*, remade especially for the gallery.

UOB Southeast Asia Gallery

Examining the art and artistic contexts of the greater Southeast Asian region, this gallery is housed in the Old Supreme Court. Keep an eye on the architecture as well as the walls while you wander around. The darkened Gallery One was once a courtroom but is now filled with art and pieces from the second half of the 19th century when most of Southeast Asia was under colonial rule. Be confronted in Gallery Three by Raden Saleh's wall-filling *Forest Fire;* however, it's the *Wounded Lion,* also by Saleh, that may give you a fright.

★ Top Tip

o The museum runs free one-hour tours through the galleries and also of the building's highlights; highly recommended. Only 20 slots are available on a first-come, first-served basis. Registration opens 20 minutes before each tour at the Tour Desk, B1 Concourse. Check the website for start times.

✕ Take a Break

If you need a quick pit stop head to **Gallery & Co.** (☎6385 6683; www.galleryand.co; 01-17 National Gallery Singapore; ◷10am-7pm Sat-Thu, to 9pm Fri) for an array of Southeast Asian–inspired dishes and desserts, plus great coffee. Once you've finished chowing down browse the eclectic range of designer books, accessories and souvenirs.

For something a little fancier head to Peranakan favourite National Kitchen by Violet Oon (p51).

Walking Tour

Colonial Singapore

In a city firmly fixed on the future, the Colonial District offers a glimpse of a romanticised era and its architectural legacies. This is the Singapore of far-flung missionaries and churches, high-society cricket clubs, Palladian-inspired buildings and the legendary Raffles Hotel. This walk takes in some of the city's most beautiful heritage buildings, swaths of soothing greenery, spectacular skyline views and even a spot of contemporary Asian art.

Walk Facts

Start Singapore Art Museum (M Bras Basah)

Finish Old Hill Street Police Station (M Fort Canning, Clarke Quay)

Length 2.6km; three to four hours

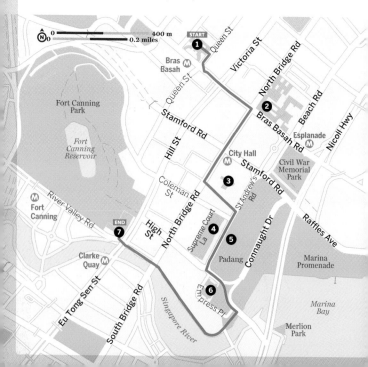

❶ Singapore Art Museum

The **Singapore Art Museum** (SAM; ☎6589 9580; www.singapore artmuseum.sg; 71 Bras Basah Rd) occupies a former Catholic boys school. Original features include the shuttered windows, ceramic floor tiles and inner quadrangle. The central dome and arcade portico were early 20th-century additions.

❷ Raffles Hotel

Head southeast along Bras Basah Rd, passing the Renaissance-inspired Cathedral of the Good Shepherd and the English Gothic Chijmes, a convent-turned-restaurant complex. Diagonally opposite Chijmes is the legendary Raffles Hotel (p47).

❸ St Andrew's Cathedral

You'll find wedding-cake-like **St Andrew's Cathedral** (☎6337 6104; www.cathedral.org.sg; 11 St Andrew's Rd; ⏰9am-5pm) further south on North Bridge Rd. Completed in 1838, it was torn down after being struck by lightning (twice!), and rebuilt by Indian convicts in 1862. It's one of Singapore's few surviving examples of English Gothic architecture.

❹ City Hall

Built in 1928, **City Hall** (1 St Andrew's Rd) is where Lord Louis Mountbatten announced the Japanese surrender in 1945 and Lee Kuan Yew declared Singapore's independence in 1965. City Hall and the Old Supreme Court, built in 1939, now house the National Gallery Singapore (p40).

❺ Padang

Opposite City Hall is the open field of the Padang, home to the Singapore Cricket Club and Singapore Recreation Club. It was here that the invading Japanese herded the European community together before marching them off to Changi Prison.

❻ Victoria Theatre

Below where St Andrew's Rd curves to the left stand a group of colonial-era buildings, including the Victoria Theatre & Concert Hall (p57). Completed in 1862, it was originally the Town Hall. It was also one of Singapore's first Victorian Revivalist buildings.

❼ Old Hill Street Police Station

Hang a right to hit the Singapore River. The multicoloured building on the corner of Hill St is the **Old Hill Street Police Station** (formerly MICA Bldg; 140 Hill St; admission free; ⏰10am-7pm). Dubbed a 'skyscraper' when built in 1934, it's now home to a string of private contemporary art galleries.

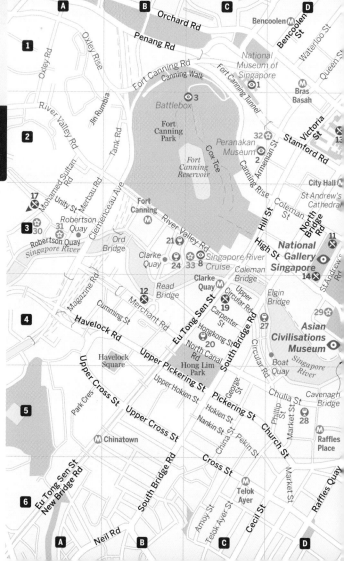

A

B Orchard Rd

C

D Bencoolen Bencoolen St

Penang Rd

1 Oxley Rd

Oxley Rise

Fort Canning Rd

Canning Walk

National Museum of Singapore

Fort Canning Tunnel 1

Waterloo St

Queen St

Jln Rumbia

Battlebox 3

Bras Basah

River Valley Rd

Fort Canning Park

Victoria St

13

2 River Valley Rd

Tank Rd

Fort Canning Reservoir

Peranakan Museum 2 32

Canning Rise

Armenian St

Stamford Rd

City Hall

St Andrew's Cathedral

Cox Tce

Mohamed Sultan Rd

Merbau Rd

Clemenceau Ave

Fort Canning

River Valley Rd

Hill St

Coleman St

North Bridge Rd

3 17 31 30

Robertson Quay

Ord Bridge

21

Singapore River Cruise

High St

National Gallery Singapore

11

14

Robertson Quay

Singapore River

Clarke Quay

24 33 8

Coleman Bridge

St Andrew's Rd

Magazine Rd

Read Bridge

Clarke Quay

Upper Circular Rd

Elgin Bridge

29

4 12

Merchant Rd

Eu Tong Sen St

19

Carpenter St

Circular Rd

27

Asian Civilisations Museum

Havelock Rd

Cumming St

20

Hongkong St

North Canal Rd

South Bridge Rd

Boat Quay

Singapore River

Havelock Square

Upper Pickering St

Hong Lim Park

George St

Chulia St

Cavenagh Bridge

5 Upper Cross St

Park Cres

Upper Hokien St

Pickering St

Hoklen St

Phillip St

Market St

28

Raffles Place

Upper Cross St

Nankin St

China St

Pekin St

Church St

6 Eu Tong Sen St

New Bridge Rd

Chinatown

South Bridge Rd

Cross St

Telok Ayer

Market St

Raffles Quay

Amoy St

Telok Ayer St

Cecil St

A Neil Rd

B

C

D

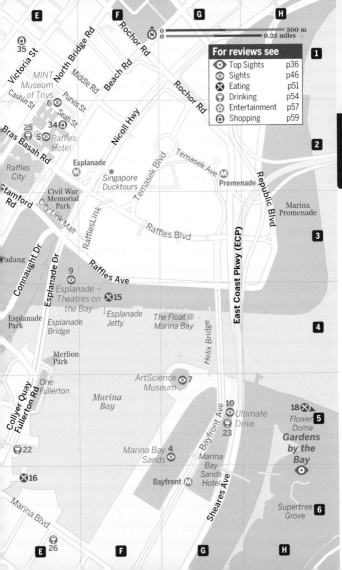

For reviews see

◉ Top Sights		p36
◎ Sights		p46
✘ Eating		p51
◗ Drinking		p54
✪ Entertainment		p57
🔒 Shopping		p59

500 m
0.25 miles

Victoria St
35

MINT
Museum
of Toys
Cashin St

North Bridge Rd
Middle Rd
Purvis St
Seah St

Rochor Rd

Beach Rd

6
25
34
5
Raffles
Hotel
Bras Basah Rd

Nicoll Hwy

Rochor Rd

Raffles
City

Esplanade

Singapore
Ducktours

Temasek Blvd
Temasek Ave

Promenade

Republic Blvd

Marina
Promenade

Civil War
Memorial
Park
City Link Mall
RafflesLink

Stamford
Rd

Raffles Blvd

Padang

Connaught Dr

Esplanade Dr

Raffles Ave

9

East Coast Pkwy (ECP)

Esplanade –
Theatres on
the Bay
15

Esplanade
Park

Esplanade
Bridge

Esplanade
Jetty

The Float @
Marina Bay

Helix Bridge

Merlion
Park

ArtScience
Museum
7

One
Fullerton

Collyer Quay
Fullerton Rd

Marina Bay

10
Ultimate
Drive
23

Bayfront Ave

18
Flower
Dome
Gardens
by the
Bay

22

16

Marina Bay
Sands
4

Bayfront

Marina
Bay
Sands
Hotel

Sheares Ave

Supertree
Grove
6

Marina Blvd

26

E   F   G   H

Sights

National Museum of Singapore

MUSEUM

1 ⊙ MAP P44, C1

Imaginative and immersive, Singapore's rebooted National Museum is good enough to warrant two visits. At once cutting edge and classical, the space ditches staid exhibits for lively multimedia galleries that bring Singapore's jam-packed biography to vivid life. It's a colourful, intimate journey, spanning ancient Malay royalty, wartime occupation, nation-building, food and fashion. Look out for interactive artwork *GoHead/GoStan: Panorama Singapura*, which offers an audiovisual trip through the city-state's many periods. Free guided tours are offered daily; check the website for times. (☑ 6332 3659; www.nationalmuseum.sg; 93 Stamford Rd; adult/child S$15/10; ☺ 10am-7pm, last admission 6.30pm; Ⓟ; Ⓜ Dhoby Ghaut, Bencoolen)

Peranakan Museum

MUSEUM

2 ⊙ MAP P44, C2

This is the best spot to explore the rich heritage of the Peranakans (Straits Chinese descendants). Thematic galleries cover various aspects of Peranakan culture, from the traditional 12-day wedding ceremony to crafts, spirituality and feasting. Look out for intricately detailed ceremonial costumes and beadwork, beautifully carved wedding beds and rare dining porcelain. An especially curious example of Peranakan fusion culture is a pair of Victorian bell jars in which statues of Christ and the Madonna are adorned with Chinese-style flowers and vines. (☑ 6332 7591; www.peranakanmuseum.org.sg; 39 Armenian St; adult/child under 7yr S$10/6, 7-9pm Fri half price; ☺ 10am-7pm, to 9pm Fri; Ⓜ City Hall, Bras Basah)

Battlebox

MUSEUM

3 ⊙ MAP P44, C2

Take a tour through the Battlebox Museum, the former command post of the British during WWII, and get lost in the eerie and deathly quiet 26-room underground complex. War veterans and Britain's Imperial War Museum helped re-create the authentic bunker environs; life-size models re-enact the fateful surrender to the Japanese on 15 February 1942. Japanese Morse codes are still etched on the walls. Due to the tour length and underground location, the museum is recommended for children over eight years old. (☑ 6338 6133; www.battlebox.com.sg; 2 Cox Tce; adult/child S$18/9; ☺ tours 1.30pm, 2.45pm & 4pm Mon, 9.45am, 11am, 1.30pm, 2.45pm & 4pm Tue-Sun; Ⓜ Dhoby Ghaut)

Marina Bay Sands

AREA

4 ⊙ MAP P44, G5

Designed by Israeli-born architect Moshe Safdie, Marina Bay Sands is a sprawling hotel, casino, mall, theatre, exhibition and museum complex. Star of the show is the **Marina Bay Sands** hotel (📞6688 8888; r from S\$550; P❄@🛜🏊), its three 55-storey towers connected by a cantilevered **SkyPark** (📞6688 8826; www.marinabaysands. com/sands-skypark; Level 57, Marina Bay Sands Hotel Tower 3; adult/child under 13yr S\$23/17; ⏱9.30am-10pm Mon-Thu, to 11pm Fri-Sun). Head up for a drink and stellar views at CÉ LA VI (p55), before catching a show at the MasterCard Theatres or doing serious damage to your credit card at the Shoppes (p59). (www. marinabaysands.com; 10 Bayfront Ave, Marina Bay; P; M Bayfront)

Raffles Hotel
NOTABLE BUILDING

5 ◉ MAP P44, E2

Although its resplendent lobby is only accessible to hotel guests,

Singapore's most iconic slumber palace is worth a quick visit for its magnificent ivory frontage, famous Sikh doorman and lush, hushed tropical grounds. It is also peppered with notable retailers and restaurants.

The hotel started life in 1887 as a modest 10-room bungalow fronting the beach (long gone thanks to land reclamation).

Behind the hotel were the Sarkies brothers, immigrants from Armenia and proprietors of two other grand colonial hotels – the Strand in Yangon (Rangoon) and the Eastern & Oriental in Penang.

The hotel's heyday began in 1899 with the opening of the main building, the same one that guests stay in today. Before long,

Marina Bay Sands hotel

Raffles Revival

Singapore's most iconic hotel has remained synonymous with Oriental luxury for over a century. Having shut her doors in late 2017, the grand old dame underwent a nearly two-year restoration and renovation (the cost of which is still under wraps, but is considerably more than her 1991 S\$160 million facelift!), which will ensure she continues to dazzle visitors with her colonial grandeur, decadence and lashings of luxury.

'Raffles' became a byword for oriental luxury – 'A legendary symbol for all the fables of the Exotic East', went the publicity blurb – and was featured in novels by Joseph Conrad and Somerset Maugham.

The famous Singapore sling was first concocted here by bartender Ngiam Tong Boon in 1915, and (far less gloriously) a Singaporean tiger, having escaped from a travelling circus nearby, was shot beneath the Billiard Room in 1902. By the 1970s the hotel had become a shabby relic, but dodged the wrecking ball in 1987 when it received National Monument designation and reopened in 1991. (☎6337 1886; www.rafflessingapore. com; 1 Beach Rd; Ⓜ City Hall, Esplanade)

MINT
Museum of Toys
MUSEUM

6 ◎ MAP P44, E2

Nostalgia rules at this slinky ode to playtime, its four skinny floors home to over 50,000 vintage toys. You'll see everything from rare Flash Gordon comics and supersonic toy guns to original Mickey Mouse dolls and oh-so-wrong golliwogs from 1930s Japan. Stock up on whimsical toys at the lobby shop or head to the adjacent **Mr Punch Rooftop Bar** (☎6339 6266; www.mrpunch. com; ◷3-11.30pm Mon-Thu, noon-1am Fri, to 11.30pm Sat, to 6.30pm Sun) to celebrate adulthood with a stiff drink. (☎6339 0660; www. emint.com; 26 Seah St; adult/child S\$15/7.50; ◷9.30am-6.30pm, last Sat of month to 9.30pm; Ⓜ City Hall, Esplanade)

ArtScience Museum
MUSEUM

7 ◎ MAP P44, G5

Designed by prolific Moshe Safdie and looking like a giant white lotus, the lily-pond-framed ArtScience Museum hosts major international travelling exhibitions in fields as varied as art, design, media, science and technology. Expect anything from explorations of deep-sea creatures to retrospectives of world-famous industrial designers. (☎6688 8826; www.marinabaysands.com; Marina

Bay Sands, 6 Bayfront Ave, Marina Bay; adult/child under 13yr from S$17/12; ◷10am-7pm, last admission 6pm; Ⓜ Bayfront)

Singapore River Cruise
BOATING

8 ◉ MAP P44, C3

This outfit runs 40-minute bumboat tours of the Singapore River and Marina Bay. The boats depart roughly every 15 minutes from various locations, including Clarke Quay, Boat Quay and Marina Bay.

A cheaper option is to catch one of the company's river taxis – commuter boats running a similar route on weekdays; see the website for stops and times. (☏ 6336 6111; www.rivercruise.com.sg; bumboat river cruise adult/child S$25/15; Ⓜ Clarke Quay)

Esplanade – Theatres on the Bay
ARTS CENTRE

9 ◉ MAP P44, E3

Singapore's S$600 million Esplanade – Theatres on the Bay offers a nonstop program of international and local performances, and free outdoor hows. Book tickets through **SISTIC** (☏ 6348 5555; www.sistic.com.sg; Level 4 Concierge, ION Orchard, 2 Orchard Turn; Ⓜ Orchard). The controversial aluminium shades – which have been compared to flies' eyes, melting honeycomb and two upturned durians – reference Asian reed-weaving geometries and maximise natural light. Since

its opening in 2002, the building has slowly but surely become accepted as part of the local landscape. (☏ 6828 8377; www.esplanade.com; 1 Esplanade Dr; ◷ box office noon-8.30pm; Ⓟ; Ⓜ Esplanade, City Hall)

Ultimate Drive
ADVENTURE SPORTS

10 ◉ MAP P44, G5

Dress to kill, then make a show of sliding into the plush interior of a high-end supercar – choose from a range of brightly coloured Ferraris and Lamborghinis – before tearing out for a spin. A taste of luxury can be yours, if only for 15 to 60 minutes. Rides also depart from Suntec City at the convention centre entrance (01-K27) between 10am and 8pm. (☏ 6688 7997; www.ultimatedrive.com; Tower 3, 01-14 Marina Bay Sands Hotel, 10 Bayfront Ave; ride as driver/passenger from S$375/300; ◷ 9am-10pm; Ⓜ Bayfront)

Singapore Ducktours

Jump into a remodelled WWII amphibious Vietnamese craft for a surprisingly informative and engaging one-hour land-and-water tour. The route focuses on Marina Bay and the Colonial District. (Map p44, F2; ☏ 6338 6877; www.ducktours.com.sg; Tower 5, 01-330 Suntec City, 3 Temasek Blvd; adult/child under 13yr S$43/33; ◷ 10am-6pm; Ⓜ Esplanade)

Architecture

Despite the wrecking-ball rampage of the 1960s and 1970s, Singapore still lays claim to a handful of heritage gems. An ever-expanding list of ambitious contemporary projects has the world watching.

Colonial Legacy

As the administrative HQ of British Malaya, Singapore gained a wave of buildings on a scale unprecedented in the colony. European aesthetics dominated, from the neoclassicism of City Hall, the Fullerton Building and the National Museum of Singapore to the Palladian-inspired Empress Building, now home to the Asian Civilisations Museum. While many other buildings adopted these styles, they were often tweaked to better suit the tropical climate, from the *porte cochère* (carriage porch) of St Andrew's Cathedral to the porticoes of the former St Joseph's Institution, now the location of the Singapore Art Museum.

Shophouses

Singapore's narrow-fronted shophouses are among its most distinctive and charming architectural trademarks. Traditionally a ground-floor business topped by one or two residential floors, these contiguous blocks roughly span six styles from the 1840s to the 1960s. The true scene stealers are those built in the so-called Late Shophouse Style, with richly detailed facades often including colourful wall tiles, stucco flourishes, pilasters and elaborately shuttered windows. Fine examples grace Koon Seng Rd in Joo Chiat (Katong).

Singapore Now

Chinese American IM Pei is behind the iconic brutalist skyscraper OCBC Centre, the silvery Raffles City, and the razor-sharp Gateway twin towers. Britain's Sir Norman Foster designed the UFO-like Expo MRT station and Supreme Court, as well as the new South Beach mixed-use development (opposite Raffles Hotel), its two curving towers sliced with densely planted sky gardens. Designed by local studio Woha, the Parkroyal on Pickering hotel features dramatic hanging gardens, while Israeli-born Moshe Safdie's Marina Bay Sands turns heads with its record-breaking, 340m-long cantilevered SkyPark.

Eating

National Kitchen by Violet Oon

PERANAKAN $$

11 MAP P44, D3

Chef Violet Oon is a national treasure, much loved for her faithful Peranakan dishes – so much so that she was chosen to open her latest venture inside Singapore's showcase National Gallery (p40). Feast on made-from-scratch beauties like sweet, spicy *kueh pie ti* (pastry cups stuffed with prawns and yam beans), dry laksa and beef *rendang*. Bookings two weeks in advance essential. (🖉9834 9935; www.violetoon.com; 02-01 National Gallery Singapore, 1 St Andrew's Rd; dishes S$15-42; ⊙noon-2.30pm & 6-9.30pm, high tea 3-4.30pm; Ⓜ City Hall)

Jumbo Seafood

CHINESE $$$

12 MAP P44, B4

If you're lusting after chilli crab – and you should be – this is a good place to indulge. The gravy is sweet and nutty, with just the right amount of chilli. Just make sure you order some *mantou* (fried buns) to soak it up. While all of Jumbo's outlets have the dish down to an art, this one has the best riverside location. (🖉6532 3435; www.jumboseafood.com.sg; 01-01/02 Riverside Point, 30 Merchant Rd; dishes from S$15, chilli crab per kg around S$88; ⊙noon-2.15pm & 6-11.15pm; Ⓜ Clarke Quay)

Whitegrass

AUSTRALIAN $$$

13 MAP P44, D2

It's all about the details in this fine-dining establishment helmed by chef-owner Sam Aisbett. From the Australian produce to the Roland Lannier steak knives and mural by local illustrator MessyMsxi (it's not wallpaper!), everything is effortlessly chic. The ever-evolving menu has Japanese and Asian influences and uses only the best produce available; it's truly a dining experience worth booking in for.

Be sure to check the cancellation fees on the website before committing to a reservation. (🖉6837 0402; www.whitegrass.com.sg; 01-26/27 Chijmes, 30 Victoria St; 2-/3-/5-/8-course lunch S$54/70/142/235, 3-/5-/8-course dinner S$116/176/265; ⊙noon-2pm Wed-Sat, 6-9.30pm Tue-Sat; 🖋; Ⓜ City Hall, Bras Basah)

Odette

FRENCH $$$

14 MAP P44, D4

Cementing its place in the upper echelons of Singapore's saturated fine-dining scene, this modern French restaurant keeps people talking with its newly minted two Michelin stars. With former **Jaan** (🖉6837 3322; www.jaan.com.sg) chef Julien Royer at the helm, menus are guided by the seasons and expertly crafted. The space is visually stunning, with a soft colour palette and floating aerial installation by local artist Dawn Ng. (🖉6385 0498; www.odette restaurant.com; 01-04 National

Gallery Singapore, 1 St Andrew's Rd; lunch/dinner from S$128/268; ⏰noon-1.30pm Tue-Sat, 7-9pm Mon-Sat; 🖊; MCity Hall)

Gluttons Bay
HAWKER $

15 ✖ MAP P44, F4

Selected by the *Makansutra Food Guide,* this row of alfresco hawker stalls is a great place to start your Singapore food odyssey. Get indecisive over classics like oyster omelette, satay, barbecue stingray and carrot cake (opt for the black version). Its central, bayside location makes it a huge hit, so head in early or late to avoid the frustrating hunt for a table. (www.makansutra.com; 01-15 Esplanade Mall, 8 Raffles Ave; dishes from S$4.50; ⏰5pm-2am Mon-Thu, to 3am Fri & Sat, 4pm-1am Sun; MEsplanade, City Hall)

Waku Ghin
JAPANESE $$$

The refinement and exquisiteness of the 10-course degustation menu by acclaimed chef Tetsuya Wakuda is nothing short of breathtaking, and the newly awarded two Michelin stars has only added to the appeal of this elusive restaurant at Marina Bay Sands (see 4 ◉ Map p44, G5). Using only the freshest ingredients, the modern Japanese-European repertoire changes daily, though the signature marinated Botan shrimp topped with sea urchin and Oscietra caviar remains a permanent show-stopper. (📞6688 8507; www.tetsuyas.com; L2-01 Shoppes at Marina Bay Sands, 2 Bayfront

Ave, access via lift A or B; degustation S$450, bar dishes S$20-60; ⏰5.30pm & 8pm seatings, bar 5.30-11.45pm; MBayfront)

Super Loco
Customs House
MEXICAN $$

16 ✖ MAP P44, E6

With a perfect harbourside location and twinkling string lights, this Mexican restaurant injects a laid-back vibe into Singapore's super-corporate CBD. Tacos are the house speciality and the *de baja* with crispy fish and chilli mango salsa is a winner; wash it down with a margarita (choose from eight flavours) while admiring the in-your-face Marina Bay Sands view. (📞6532 2090; www.super-loco.com; 01-04 Customs House, 70 Collyer Quay; dishes S$8-38, set lunch from S$35; ⏰noon-3pm & 5-10.30pm Mon-Thu, noon-11pm Fri, 5-11pm Sat; 🖊; MRaffles Place, Downtown)

Common Man
Coffee Roasters
CAFE $$

17 ✖ MAP P44, A3

While this airy, industrial-cool cafe roasts and serves top-class coffee, it also serves seriously scrumptious grub. Produce is super fresh and the combinations simple yet inspired, from all-day brekkie winners like filo-wrapped soft-boiled eggs paired with creamy hummus, feta, olives, cucumber and tomato, to a lunchtime quinoa salad with grilled sweet potato, spinach, mint, coriander, goat cheese and honey-raisin yoghurt. (📞6836 4695;

Quays of the City

The stretch of riverfront that separates the Colonial District from the CBD is known as the Quays.

Boat Quay (Map p44, D4; M Raffles Place, Clarke Quay) Boat Quay was once Singapore's centre of commerce, and remained an important economic area into the 1960s. The area became a major entertainment district in the 1990s, filled with touristy bars, shops and menu-clutching touts. Discerning punters ditch these for the growing number of clued-in cafes and drinking dens dotting the streets behind the main strip.

Clarke Quay (Map p44, B3; M Clarke Quay, Fort Canning) How much time you spend in Clarke Quay really depends upon your personal taste in aesthetics. If pastel hues, Dr Seuss–style design and lad-and-ladette hang-outs are your schtick, you'll be in your element. Fans of understated cool, however, should steer well clear.

Robertson Quay (Map p44, A3; M Clarke Quay, Fort Canning) At the furthest reach of the river, Robertson Quay was once used for the storage of goods. Now some of the old *godown* (warehouses) have found new purposes as bars and members-only party places. The vibe here is more 'grown up' than Clarke Quay, attracting a 30-plus crowd generally more interested in wining, dining and conversation than getting hammered to Top 40 hits.

www.commonmancoffeeroasters.com; 22 Martin Rd; mains S$14-29; ⏰7.30am-5pm Mon-Fri, to 5.30pm Sat & Sun; 🛜🍽; M Fort Canning)

Satay by the Bay HAWKER $

18 ✗ MAP P44, H5

Gardens by the Bay's own hawker centre has an enviable location, alongside Marina Bay and far from the roar of city traffic. Especially evocative at night, it's known for its satay, best devoured under open skies on the spacious wooden deck. The bulk of the food stalls are open 11am to 10.30pm. (📞6538 9956; www.sataybythebay.com.sg; Gardens by the Bay, 18 Marina Gardens Dr; dishes from S$4; ⏰stall hours vary, drinks stall 24hr; M Bayfront)

Song Fa Bak Kut Teh CHINESE $

19 ✗ MAP P44, C4

If you need a hug, this cult-status eatery delivers with its *bak kut teh*. Literally 'meat bone tea', it's a soothing concoction of fleshy pork ribs simmered in a peppery broth of herbs, spices and whole garlic cloves. The ribs are sublimely sweet and melt-in-the-mouth, and staff will happily refill your bowl with broth. (6533 6128; www.songfa.com.sg; 11 New Bridge Rd; dishes S$3.20-11.50; 9am-9.15pm Tue-Sun; M Clarke Quay)

Drinking

Smoke & Mirrors
BAR

Oozing style, this rooftop bar (see 11 ✕ Map p44, D3) offers one of the best views of Singapore. Perched on the top of the National Gallery, the vista looks out over the Padang (p43) to Marina Bay Sands (p46) and is flanked by skyscrapers on either side. Arrive before sunset so you can sit, drink in hand, and watch the city transition from day to night. Book ahead. (9234 8122; www. smokeandmirrors.com.sg; 06-01 National Gallery Singapore, 1 St Andrew's Rd; 3pm-1am Mon-Thu, to 2am Fri, noon-2am Sat, to 1am Sun; M City Hall)

28 HongKong Street
COCKTAIL BAR

20 MAP P44, C4

Softly lit 28HKS plays hide and seek inside an unmarked 1960s shophouse. Slip inside and into a slinky scene of cosy booths and passionate mixologists turning grog into greatness. Marked with their alcohol strength, cocktails are seamless and sublime, among them the fruity '93 'til Infinity' with pisco, pineapple, lime and

Clarke Quay (p53)

cypress. House-barrelled classics, hard-to-find beers and lip-smacking grub seal the deal.

Email findus@28hks.com for reservations. (www.28hks.com; 28 Hongkong St; ☉5.30pm-1am Mon-Thu, to 3am Fri & Sat; Ⓜ Clarke Quay)

Zouk
CLUB

21 🚇 MAP P44, B3

After a massive farewell to Zouk's original location, this legendary club has settled in to its new home in pumping Clarke Quay. Drawing some of the world's biggest DJs and Singapore's see-and-be-seen crowd, this is the place to go to if you want to let loose. Choose between the main two-level club with pumping dance floor and insane lighting, or the hip-hop-centric, graffiti-splashed Phuture. (📞6738 2988; www.zoukclub.com; 3C River Valley Rd; women/men from S$30/35 redeemable for drinks; ☉Zouk 10pm-4am Fri, Sat & Wed, Phuture 10pm-3am Wed & Fri, to 2am Thu, to 4am Sat; Ⓜ Clarke Quay, Fort Canning)

Landing Point
LOUNGE

22 🚇 MAP P44, E5

For a decadent high tea, it's hard to beat the one at this chichi water-side lounge. Book ahead (one week for weekdays, one month for weekends), style up, and head in on an empty stomach. Steaming pots of TWG tea are paired with delectable morsels like truffled-egg sandwiches, melt-in-your-mouth quiche, brioche buns

topped with duck and blueberries, and caramel-filled dark-chocolate tarts. (📞6333 8388; www.fullerton hotels.com; Fullerton Bay Hotel, 80 Collyer Quay; high tea per adult/child under 12yr S$48/24; ☉9am-midnight Sun-Thu, to 1am Fri & Sat, high tea 3-5.30pm Mon-Fri, noon-2pm & 3-5pm Sat & Sun; 🛜; Ⓜ Raffles Place)

CÉ LA VI SkyBar
BAR

23 🚇 MAP P44, G5

Perched on Marina Bay Sands' cantilevered SkyPark, this bar offers a jaw-dropping panorama of the Singapore skyline and beyond. A dress code kicks in from 6pm (no shorts, singlets or flip-flops) and live DJ sets pump from late afternoon. Tip: skip the S$23 entry fee to the SkyPark Observation Deck (p47) – come here, order a cocktail and enjoy the same view. (📞6508 2188; www.sg.celavi.com; Level 57, Marina Bay Sands Hotel Tower 3, 10 Bayfront Ave; admission S$20, redeemable on food or drinks; ☉noon-late; Ⓜ Bayfront)

Fleek
CLUB

24 🚇 MAP P44, B3

When you're 'on fleek' you're at the pinnacle and this shrine to hip-hop is just that. Tiny compared to neighbouring Clarke Quay megaclubs, Fleek packs a megapunch with a potent formula of pumping beats, cheap drinks and an off-the-hook dance floor. It's the place you go to lose yourself in the music; the Thursday night S$10 house pours will help you on your way. (☎8808 0854; www.facebook.com/fleeksg; 01-10, 3C River Valley Rd; ⏰6pm-4am Wed-Sat; Ⓜ Clarke Quay, Fort Canning)

Long Bar
BAR

25 Ⓜ MAP P44, E2

Famous the world over, the Raffles Hotel Long Bar is the very place that bartender Ngiam Tong Boon invented the now legendary Singapore sling in 1915. Having undergone a sensitive restoration, the colonial plantation-inspired bar reopened in September 2018. Thankfully the beloved sling remains the same, as does the tradition of discarding peanut shells directly on the floor. (☎6337 1886; www.rafflessingapore.com; Raffles Hotel, 1 Beach Rd; ⏰11am-11pm; Ⓜ City Hall, Esplanade)

Level 33
MICROBREWERY

26 Ⓜ MAP P44, E6

In a country obsessed with unique selling points, this brewery takes the cake – no, keg. Claiming to be the world's highest 'urban craft brewery', Level 33 brews its own lager, pale ale, stout, porter and wheat beer – order the tasting paddle to try them all. It's all yours to slurp alfresco with a marvellous view over Marina Bay. (☎6834 3133; www.level33.com.sg; Level 33, Marina Bay Financial Tower 1, 8 Marina Blvd; ⏰11.30am-midnight Mon-Thu, to 2am Fri & Sat, noon-midnight Sun; 🛜; Ⓜ Downtown)

Headquarters by the Council
CLUB

27 Ⓜ MAP P44, C4

Don't let the unassuming facade of this shophouse fool you. Follow the just audible thumping beat and look for the Morse code on the pillar till you find yourself joining one of Singapore's hottest dance floors. Pumping out mainly techno and house, with a dash of disco, this is the place to head to if you want to dance, dance, dance. (☎8125 8880; www.facebook.com/headquarters.sg; Level 2, 66 Boat Quay; ⏰6pm-3am Wed-Fri, 10pm-4am Sat; Ⓜ Clarke Quay)

1-Altitude Rooftop Gallery & Bar
BAR

28 Ⓜ MAP P44, D5

Wedged across a triangle-shaped deck 282m above street level, this is the world's highest alfresco bar, its 360-degree panorama taking in soaring towers, colonial landmarks and a ship-clogged sea. Women enjoy free entry and all-night S$10 martinis on Wednesday, while Get Busy Thursday pumps out hip-hop and R&B hits. Dress up: no shorts or open shoes, gents. (☎6438 0410; www.1-altitude.com; Level 63, 1 Raffles Pl; admission incl 1 drink S$30, from 9pm S$35; ⏰6pm-2am Sun-Tue, to 3am Thu, to 4am Wed, Fri & Sat; Ⓜ Raffles Place)

Singlish, lah!

While there isn't a Singlish grammar as such, there are definite characteristics. Verb tenses tend to be nonexistent. Past, present and future are indicated instead by time indicators, so in Singlish it's 'I go tomorrow' or 'I go yesterday'. Long stress is placed on the last syllable of phrases, so that the standard English 'government' becomes 'guvva-men'.

Words ending in consonants are often syncopated and vowels are often distorted. A Chinese-speaking taxi driver might not immediately understand that you want to go to Perak Rd, since they know it as 'Pera Roh'.

A typical exchange might – confusingly – go something like this: '*Eh*, this Sunday you going *cheong* (party), *anot*? No, *ah*? Why like that? Don't be so boring, *lah*!' Prepositions and pronouns are dropped, word order is flipped, phrases are clipped short and stress and cadence are unconventional, to say the least.

The particle *lah* is often tagged on to the end of sentences for emphasis, as in 'No good, *lah*'. Requests or questions may be marked with a tag ending, since direct questioning can be rude. As a result, questions that are formed to be more polite often come across to Westerners as rude. 'Would you like a beer?' becomes 'You wan beer or not?'

For more, check out the Coxford Singlish Dictionary on the satirical website Talking Cock (www.talkingcock.com).

Entertainment

Singapore Symphony Orchestra
CLASSICAL MUSIC

29 ⭐ MAP P44, D4

The neo-classical **Victoria Theatre & Concert Hall** (☏6908 8810; www.vtvch.com; ⏰10am-9pm) is home to Singapore's well-respected flagship orchestra, which makes its performing home at the 1800-seat state-of-the-art Esplanade – Theatres on the Bay (p49). It plays at least weekly; check the website or SISTIC (p49) for details and book ahead. There is a box office on-site. Student and senior (over 55) discounts available; kids under six years not permitted. (SSO; ☏6602 4245; www.sso.org.sg; 01-02 Victoria Concert Hall, 9 Empress Pl; ⏰box office 9am-6.30pm Mon-Fri, 1hr before performances at Victoria Concert Hall; MRaffles Place, City Hall)

TheatreWorks

THEATRE

30 ⭐ MAP P44, A3

One of the more experimental theatre companies in Singapore, TheatreWorks is led by enigmatic artistic director Ong Keng Sen. A mix of fresh local work and international collaborations, performances are housed in the company's headquarters, a former rice warehouse just off Robertson Quay. See the website for updates. (📞6737 7213; www.theatreworks.org.sg; 72-13 Mohamed Sultan Rd; Ⓜ Fort Canning)

Singapore Repertory Theatre

THEATRE

31 ⭐ MAP P44, A3

Based at the KC Arts Centre but also performing at other venues, the SRT produces international repertory standards as well as modern Singaporean plays. Check the website for upcoming productions. (SRT; 📞6221 5585; www.srt.com.sg; KC Arts Centre, 20 Merbau Rd; Ⓜ Fort Canning)

Timbrè @ The Substation

LIVE MUSIC

32 ⭐ MAP P44, D2

Young ones are content to queue for seats at this popular live-music venue, whose rotating roster features local bands and singer-songwriters playing anything from pop and rock to folk. Hungry punters can fill up on soups, salads, tapas and fried standbys like buffalo wings and truffle fries. The weekday liquid buffet (S$19) offers an hour of free-flow on selected drinks starting at 5pm. (📞6338 8030; www.timbre.com.sg; 45 Armenian St; ⏰5pm-1am Mon-Thu, to 3am Fri & Sat; Ⓜ City Hall, Bras Basah)

Crazy Elephant

LIVE MUSIC

33 ⭐ MAP P44, C3

Anywhere that bills itself as 'crazy' should set the alarm bells ringing, but you won't hear them once you're inside. This touristy, graffiti-lined rock bar is beery, blokey and loud. Music ranges from rock to deep funky blues. Happy hour runs 5pm to 9pm and the musicians hit the stage from 9pm Monday to Saturday and from 8pm Sunday. (📞6337 7859; www.crazyelephant.sg; 01-03/04 3E River Valley Rd; ⏰5pm-2am Tue-Thu & Sun, to 1am Mon, to 3am Fri & Sat; Ⓜ Clarke Quay, Fort Canning)

Shoppes at Marina Bay Sands

ARIYAPHOL JIWALAK/SHUTTERSTOCK ©

Shopping

Raffles Hotel Gift Shop

GIFTS & SOUVENIRS

34 🔒 MAP P44, E2

It might sound like a tourist trap, but the Raffles Hotel gift shop is a good spot for quality souvenirs, whatever your budget. Pick up anything from vintage hotel posters to handcrafted silk cushions, and branded Raffles stationery, tea sets and toiletries. (📞6337 1886; www.rafflessingapore.com; 1 Beach Rd; 🕙9am-8pm; Ⓜ City Hall, Esplanade)

Shoppes at Marina Bay Sands

MALL

From Miu Miu pumps and Prada frocks to Boggi Milano blazers, this sprawling temple of aspiration (see 4 ◎ Map p44, G5) gives credit cards a thorough workout. Despite being one of Singapore's largest luxury malls, it's relatively thin on crowds – great if you're not a fan of the Orchard Rd pandemonium. The world's first floating Louis Vuitton store is also here, right on Marina Bay. (📞6688 8868; www.marinabaysands.com; 10 Bayfront Ave; 🕙10.30am-11pm Sun-Thu, to 11.30pm Fri & Sat; 📶; Ⓜ Bayfront)

Free Concerts

If you're hankering for wallet-friendly diversions, Esplanade – Theatres on the Bay (p49) offers free live performances throughout the week, and the Singapore Symphony Orchestra (p57) performs free at the Singapore Botanic Gardens (p102) monthly. Check online for details.

Kapok

GIFTS & SOUVENIRS

35 🔒 MAP P44, E1

Inside the National Design Centre, Kapok showcases beautifully designed products from Singapore and beyond. Restyle your world with local jewellery from Amado Gudek and Lorem Ipsum Store and a flattering dress by GINLEE Studio. Imports include anything from seamless Italian wallets to British striped tees and Spanish backpacks. When you're shopped out, recharge at the on-site cafe. (📞9060 9107; www.ka-pok.com; 01-05 National Design Centre, 111 Middle Rd; 🕙11am-8pm; Ⓜ Bugis, Bras Basah)

Little India & Kampong Glam

Little India is Singapore trapped in its gritty past – it's frenetic, messy and fun. Spice traders spill their wares across its five-foot ways and Indian labourers swarm into the area each weekend. Kampong Glam, the former home of the local sultan, is an eclectic mix of Islamic stores and eateries, hipster bars and boutiques.

The Short List

○ **Lagnaa Barefoot Dining (p71)** *Braving your choice of mouth-burning spice levels at this famous curry house.*

○ **Tekka Centre (p73)** *Shopping for saris followed by authentic street eats at the downstairs hawker market.*

○ **Sri Veeramakaliamman Temple (p67)** *Experiencing this atmospheric Hindu temple.*

○ **Sifr Aromatics (p79)** *Customising the perfect fragrance at this perfume lab.*

Getting There & Around

Ⓜ Little India MRT station is right by the Tekka Centre. You can walk here from Rochor, Jalan Besar, Bugis and Farrer Park MRT stations.

Ⓜ Bugis is best for Kampong Glam, and the busy, up-and-coming Jalan Besar area (clustered just south of Lavender St) is easily reached from Bendemeer, Lavender or Farrer Park MRT stations.

Neighbourhood Map on p64

Sultan Mosque (p66) RONNIE CHUA/SHUTTERSTOCK ©

Walking Tour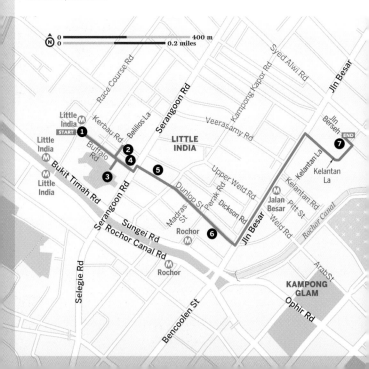

A Stroll in Little India

Loud, colourful and refreshingly raffish, Little India stands in contrast to the more sanitised parts of the city. Dive into a gritty, pungent wonderland of dusty grocery shops, gold and sari traders, haggling Indian families and heady Hindu temples. Jumble them all together with a gut-busting booty of fiery eateries and you have Singapore's most hypnotic, electrifying urban experience.

Walk Facts

Start Corner of Buffalo and Race Course Rds (Ⓜ Little India)

Finish Sungei Road Laksa (Ⓜ Jalan Besar)

Length 1.5km; two hours with stops

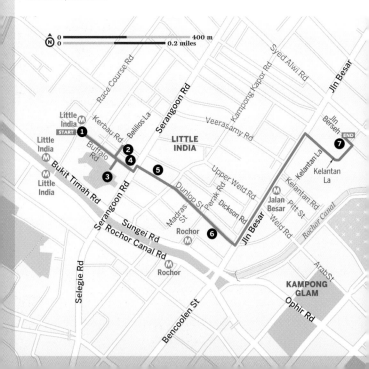

❶ Buffalo Road

Plunge into subcontinental Singapore on Buffalo Rd, a bustling strip packed with brightly coloured facades, Indian produce shops and garland stalls. Flowers used to make the garlands are highly symbolic: both the lotus and the white jasmine spell purity, while the yellow marigold denotes peace.

❷ Tan House

As you walk up Buffalo Rd towards Serangoon Rd, look for an alley on your left leading to Kerbau Rd. Take a quick detour down it and be dazzled by Tan House, quite possibly Singapore's most colourful building. When you're Instagrammed out, head back to Buffalo Rd.

❸ Tekka Centre Wet Market

If it's morning, scour the wet market inside Tekka Centre (p73), where locals battle it out for the city's freshest produce. It's an intense place, stocking everything from fresh yoghurt to dried curry spices. If you're after a sari, the top floor has a swarm of vendors.

❹ Nalli

For quality cotton and silk saris, many locals head to **Nalli** (☑6299 3949; www.nallisingapore.com.sg; 10 Buffalo Rd; ⏱10am-9.30pm Mon-Sat, to 7.30pm Sun) directly opposite the Tekka Centre. It's a small, industrious shop where you can pick up cotton saris for as little as S$40. If money isn't an issue, consider opting for a beautiful silk version, which usually go for between S$100 and S$1000.

❺ Thandapani Co

Slip into Dunlop St and look for **Thandapani Co** (☑6292 3163; 124 Dunlop St; ⏱9.30am-9.30pm). Adorned with hessian bags packed with chillies, fennel seeds and other Indian staples, this grocery shop is considered one of the city's best spice vendors and stocks ingredients you won't find elsewhere.

❻ Abdul Gafoor Mosque

Equally enticing is **Abdul Gafoor Mosque** (☑6295 4209; www.facebook.com/masjidabdulgafoor; 41 Dunlop St; admission free; ⏱10am-noon & 2-4pm Sat-Thu, 2.30-4pm Fri), with its peculiar mix of Islamic and Victorian architecture. Completed in 1910, it features an elaborate sundial crowning its main entrance; each of the 25 rays is decorated with Arabic calligraphy denoting the names of 25 prophets.

❼ Sungei Road Laksa

End your local adventure with a cheap, steamy fix at **Sungei Road Laksa** (www.sungeiroadlaksa.com.sg; 01-100, Block 27, Jln Berseh; laksa S$3; ⏱9am-6pm, closed 1st & 3rd Wed of the month). The fragrant, savoury, coconut-base soup enjoys a cult following, and only charcoal is used to keep the precious gravy warm. To avoid the lunchtime crowds, head in before 11.30am or after 2pm.

Little India & Kampong Glam

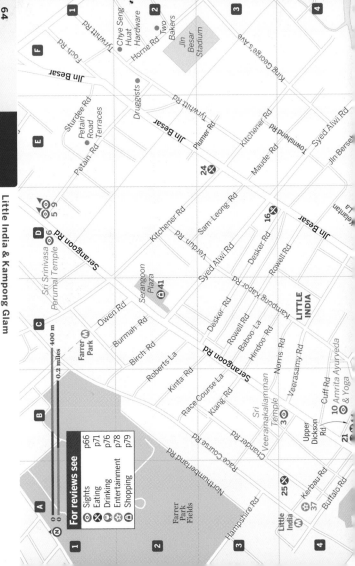

Chye Seng Huat Hardware

Two Bakers

Jln Besar Stadium

Tyrwhitt Rd

Foch Rd

Horne Rd

King George's Ave

Jln Besar

Sturdee Rd

Petain Road Terraces

Petain Rd

Druggists

Jln Besar

Tyrwhitt Rd

Plumer Rd

Kitchener Rd

Townshend Rd

Syed Alwi Rd

Jln Berseh

Maude Rd

Jln Besar

Jln Kelantan La

24 ✗

Kitchener Rd

Sam Leong Rd

Verdun Rd

Sri Srinivasa Perumal Temple

Serangoon Rd

5 9

6

Desker Rd

Syed Alwi Rd

16 ✗

Rowell Rd

Serangoon Plaza

41

Owen Rd

Burmah Rd

Birch Rd

Roberts La

Kinta Rd

Desker Rd

Kampong Kapor Rd

Rowell Rd

Baboo La

Hindoo Rd

Norris Rd

LITTLE INDIA

Farrer Park M

Race Course La

Klang Rd

Sri Veeramakaliamman Temple

3

Veerasamy Rd

Cuff Rd

Amrita Ayurveda & Yoga

10

Chander Rd

Upper Dickson Rd

21

Race Course Rd

Northumberland Rd

Hampshire Rd

Farrer Park Fields

25 ✗

Kerbau Rd

Little India M

37

Buffalo Rd

For reviews see

👁 Sights	p66
✗ Eating	p71
🍷 Drinking	p76
✪ Entertainment	p78
🛍 Shopping	p79

0.2 miles

400 m

N

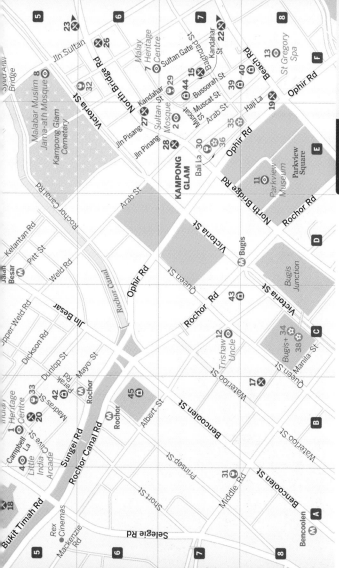

Little India & Kampong Glam

Sights

Indian Heritage Centre

MUSEUM

1  MAP P64, B5

Delve into the origins and heritage of Singapore's Indian community at this S$12 million state-of-the-art museum. Divided into five themes, its hundreds of historical and cultural artefacts, maps, archival footage and multimedia displays explore everything from early interactions between South Asia and Southeast Asia to Indian cultural traditions and the contributions of Indian Singaporeans to the development of the island nation. Among the more extraordinary objects is a 19th-century Chettinad doorway, intricately adorned with

5000 minute carvings. (☎6291 1601; www.indianheritage.org.sg; 5 Campbell Lane; adult/child under 6yr S$6/free; ☺10am-7pm Tue-Thu, to 8pm Fri & Sat, to 4pm Sun; Ⓜ Little India, Jalan Besar)

Sultan Mosque

MOSQUE

2  MAP P64, E7

Seemingly pulled from the pages of the *Arabian Nights*, Singapore's largest mosque is nothing short of enchanting, designed in the Saracenic style and topped by a golden dome. It was originally built in 1825 with the aid of a grant from Raffles and the East India Company, after Raffles' treaty with the sultan of Singapore allowed the Malay leader to retain sovereignty over the area. In 1928 the original mosque was replaced by

Sri Veeramakaliamman Temple

the present magnificent building, designed by an Irish architect.

Non-Muslims are asked to refrain from entering the prayer hall at any time, and all visitors are expected to be dressed suitably (cloaks are available at the entrance). Pointing cameras at people during prayer time is never appropriate. (📞6293 4405; www. sultanmosque.sg; 3 Muscat St; admission free; ⏱10am-noon & 2-4pm Sat-Thu, 2.30-4pm Fri; Ⓜ Bugis)

Sri Veeramakaliamman Temple
HINDU TEMPLE

3 ◎ MAP P64, B4

Little India's most colourful, visually stunning temple is dedicated to the ferocious goddess Kali, depicted wearing a garland of skulls, ripping out the insides of her victims, and sharing more tranquil family moments with her sons Ganesh and Murugan. The bloodthirsty consort of Shiva has always been popular in Bengal, the birthplace of the labourers who built the structure in 1881. The temple is at its most evocative during each of the four daily *puja* (prayer) sessions. (📞6295 4538; www.sriveeramakaliamman. com; 141 Serangoon Rd; admission free; ⏱5.30am-12.30pm & 4-9.30pm; Ⓜ Little India, Jalan Besar)

Little India Arcade
MARKET

4 ◎ MAP P64, B5

This modest but colourful area of wall-to-wall shops, pungent aromas and Hindi film music is

Petain Road Terraces

Between Jln Besar and Sturdee Rd is an extraordinary row of lavishly decorated double-storey **terraces** (Map p64, E1; Petain Rd; Ⓜ Farrer Park, Bendemeer) dating back to the 1920s. They're a gasp-inducing explosion of colour, from the floral-motif ceramic wall tiles to the pillar bas-reliefs adorned with flowers, birds and trees. The hyper-ornate decoration is typical of what's known as Late Shophouse Style.

a welcome contrast to the prim modernity of many parts of the city. The arcade has an inside section as well as shops running along Campbell Lane. It's the place to come to pick up that framed print of Krishna you've always wanted, eat great food and watch street-side cooks fry chapatis. (📞6295 5998; www.littleindiaarcade.com.sg; 48 Serangoon Rd; ⏱9am-10pm; Ⓜ Little India, Jalan Besar)

Sri Vadapathira Kaliamman Temple
HINDU TEMPLE

5 ◎ MAP P64, D1

Dedicated to Kaliamman, the Destroyer of Evil, this South Indian temple began life in 1870 as a modest shrine but underwent a significant facelift in 1969 to transform it into the beauty standing today. The carvings here – particularly on the *vimana* (domed structure within the temple) – are among the best temple artwork you'll see anywhere in Singapore. (📞6298 5053; www. srivadapathirakali.org; 555 Serangoon Rd; admission free; ⏰6am-9pm; Ⓜ️Farrer Park, Bendemeer)

Sri Srinivasa Perumal Temple
HINDU TEMPLE

6 ◉ MAP P64, D1

Dedicated to Vishnu, this temple dates from 1855, but the striking, 20m-tall *gopuram* (tower) is a S$300,000 1966 add-on. Inside are statues of Vishnu, Lakshmi and Andal, and Vishnu's bird-mount Garuda. The temple is the starting point for a colourful, wince-inducing street parade during the Thaipusam festival: to show their devotion, many participants pierce their bodies with hooks and skewers. (📞6298 5771; www.sspt. org.sg; 397 Serangoon Rd; admission free; ⏰6am-noon & 6-9pm Sun-Mon, 5.30am-12.30pm & 5.30-9.30pm Sat; Ⓜ️Farrer Park, Bendemeer)

Malay Heritage Centre
MUSEUM

7 ◉ MAP P64, F6

The Kampong Glam area is the historic seat of Malay royalty, resident here before the arrival of Raffles, and the *istana* (palace) on this site was built for the last sultan of Singapore, Ali Iskandar Shah, between 1836 and 1843. It's now a museum, its galleries exploring Malay-Singaporean culture and history, from the early migration of traders

to Kampong Glam to the development of Malay-Singaporean film, theatre, music and publishing.

Free guided tours run at 2pm Tuesdays, Thursdays and Saturdays. (📞6391 0450; www.malay heritage.org.sg; 85 Sultan Gate; adult/child under 6yr $6/free; ⏰10am-6pm Tue-Sun; Ⓜ️Bugis)

Malabar Muslim Jama-ath Mosque
MOSQUE

8 ◉ MAP P64, F5

Architecture goes easy-wipe at the golden-domed Malabar Muslim Jama-ath Mosque, a curious creation clad entirely in striking blue geometric tiles. This is the only mosque on the island dedicated to Malabar Muslims from the South Indian state of Kerala, and though the building was commenced in 1956, it wasn't officially opened until 1963 due to cash-flow problems. The better-late-than-never motif continued with the tiling, which was only completed in 1995. (📞6294 3862; www.malabar.org.sg; 471 Victoria St; admission free; ⏰noon-1pm & 2-4pm Sat-Thu, from 2.30pm Fri; Ⓜ️Bugis, Lavender)

Sakya Muni Buddha Gaya Temple
BUDDHIST TEMPLE

9 ◉ MAP P64, D1

Dominating this temple is a 15m-tall, 300-tonne Buddha. Keeping him company is an eclectic cast of deities, including Kuan Yin (Guan Yin; the Chinese goddess of mercy) and, interestingly, the Hindu deities

Banksy, Asian-Style

Street artist Ernest Zacharevic (www.ernestzacharevic.com) has been dubbed the Malaysian Banksy. Born in Lithuania and based in Penang, the twenty-something artist has garnered a global following for his fantastically playful, interactive street art. From Stavanger to Singapore, his murals often incorporate real-life props, whether old bicycles, wooden chairs or even the moss growing out of cracks. In one small work opposite the Malabar Muslim Jama-ath Mosque (Map p64, F5) two exhilarated kids freewheel it on a pair of 3D supermarket trolleys. To the right, a young boy somersaults out of a box, while further south, on the corner of Victoria St and Jln Pisang, a giant girl caresses a snoozing lion cub.

Brahma and Ganesh. The yellow tigers flanking the entrance symbolise protection and vitality, while the huge mother-of-pearl Buddha footprint to your left as you enter is reputedly a replica of the footprint on top of Adam's Peak in Sri Lanka.

The footprint's 108 auspicious marks distinguish a Buddha foot from any other 2m-long foot. The temple, which stands opposite the Taoist **Leong San See Temple** (📞6298 9371; 371 Race Course Rd; admission free; ⏲7.30am-5pm), was founded by a Thai monk in 1927. (Temple of 1000 Lights; 366 Race Course Rd; admission free; ⏲8am-4.30pm; Ⓜ Farrer Park, Bendemeer)

Amrita Ayurveda & Yoga
MASSAGE

10 ◎ MAP P64, B4

If Little India's hyperactive energy leaves you frazzled, revive the Indian way with an Ayurvedic (traditional Indian medicine) massage at this modest, friendly place.

Treatments include the highly popular Abhyangam (synchronised massage using medicated oils) and the deeply relaxing Shirodhara (warm oil poured over the forehead). Yoga classes are also on offer. (📞6299 0642; www.amrita.sg; 11 Upper Dickson Rd; 30min massage from S$35; ⏲9am-9pm Mon-Sat, to 3pm Sun; Ⓜ Little India, Jalan Besar)

Parkview Museum
MUSEUM

11 ◎ MAP P64, E8

This cavernous 1500-sq-metre contemporary art museum was opened in 2017 by the Parkview Group, owners of the iconic art-deco building Parkview Square in which the museum is housed. Designed to enrich the local art scene and encourage the integration and appreciation of art in everyday life, it features contemporary artworks by international artists.

Dress to impress and head to Atlas (p76), the extravagant lobby bar.(☎6799 6971; www.parkview-museum.com; Level 3, Parkview Sq, 600 North Bridge Rd; admission free; ⏱noon-7pm; Ⓜ Bugis)

Trishaw Uncle
TOURS

12 ◉ MAP P64, C7

Hop on a trishaw for an old-fashioned ride through China-town, Kampong Glam or Little India. The Chinatown tour also takes in the Singapore River and will drop you off at the Chinatown Heritage Centre (p138), instead of back at the tour starting point. You'll find the trishaw terminal on Queen St, between the Fu Lu Shou Complex and Albert Centre Market and Food Centre. (☎6337 7111; www.trishawuncle.com.sg; Albert Mall Trishaw Park, Queen St;

adult/child 30min tour from S$39/29, 45min tour S$49/39; Ⓜ Bugis)

St Gregory Spa
SPA

13 ◉ MAP P64, F8

The St Gregory group is a major player in the relaxation stakes, with three facilities in Singapore. This tranquil branch is at the Parkroyal hotel, its forest-inspired design a dreamy backdrop for treatments ranging from Swedish massage, wraps and milk baths to traditional Chinese therapies and oil-based Ayurvedic massage. (☎6505 5755; www.stgregoryspa.com; Level 4, Parkroyal, 7500 Beach Rd; treatments S$45-300; ⏱10am-10pm Mon-Fri, 9am-9pm Sat & Sun; Ⓜ Bugis, Nicoll Hwy)

Trishaw Uncle

Eating

Lagnaa Barefoot Dining

INDIAN $$

14 ❌ MAP P64, B4

You can choose your level of spice at friendly Lagnaa: level three denotes standard spiciness, level four significant spiciness, and anything above admirable bravery. Whatever you opt for, you're in for finger-licking-good homestyle cooking from both ends of Mother India, devoured at Western seating downstairs or on floor cushions upstairs. If you're indecisive, order chef Kaesavan's famous Threadfin fish curry. (6296 1215; www.lagnaa.com; 6 Upper Dickson Rd; dishes S$8-22; 11.30am-10.30pm; ; Little India)

Cicheti

ITALIAN $$

15 ❌ MAP P64, F7

Cool-kid Cicheti is a slick, friendly, buzzing scene of young-gun pizzaioli, chic diners and seductive, contemporary Italian dishes made with hand-picked market produce. Tuck into beautifully charred wood-fired pizzas, made-from-scratch pasta and standouts like *polpette di carne* (slow-cooked meatballs). Book early in the week if heading in on a Friday or Saturday night. (6292 5012; www.cicheti.com; 52 Kandahar St; pizzas S$18-25, mains S$22-56; noon-2.30pm & 6.30-10.30pm Mon-Fri, 6-10.30pm Sat; Bugis, Nicoll Hwy)

Swee Choon Tim Sum

DIM SUM $

16 ❌ MAP P64, D3

What started as a single shophouse dim-sum restaurant in 1962, Swee Choon has grown to consume all the floorspace, sidewalk and back alley of four connected shophouses. It's still bursting at the seams, but don't be put off by the throngs of waiting customers as the line is well organised and moves quickly. The salted egg-yolk custard buns are like nothing you've ever tasted. (6225 7788; www.sweechoon.com; 183-191 Jln Besar; dishes S$1.40-9; 11am-2.30pm & 6pm-6am Mon, Wed-Sat, 10am-3pm & 6pm-6am Sun; Jalan Besar, Rochor)

QS269 Food House

HAWKER $

17 ❌ MAP P64, B8

This is not so much a 'food house' as a loud, crowded undercover laneway lined with cult-status stalls. Work up a sweat with a bowl of award-winning coconut-curry noodle soup from **Ah Heng** (www.facebook.com/ahhengchickencurrynoodles; soup S$4.50-6.50; 9.30am-10pm) or join the queue at **New Rong Liang Ge** (dishes from S$2.50; 9am-8pm, closed 1st Wed of the month), with succulent roast-duck dishes that draw foodies from across the city. The laneway is down the side of the building. (Block 269B, Queen St; dishes from S$2.50; stall hours vary; Bugis)

The Singaporean Table

Food is one of Singapore's greatest drawcards, the nation's melting pot of cultures creating one of the world's most diverse, drool-inducing culinary landscapes.

Chinese

Thank the Hainanese for Hainanese chicken rice (steamed fowl and rice cooked in chicken stock, and served with a clear soup, slices of cucumber and ginger, chilli and soy dips), and the Hokkiens for hokkien mee (yellow Hokkien noodles with prawn) and char kway teow (stir-fried noodles with cockles, Chinese sausage and dark sauces). Teochew cuisine is famed for its rice porridge, while Cantonese classics include won-ton soup.

Indian

South Indian's hot flavours dominate. Tuck into thali, a combination of rice, curries, *rasam* (hot, sour soup) and dessert served on a banana leaf. Leave room for *roti prata* (fried flat bread served with curry sauce), *masala dosa* (thin pancake filled with spiced potato and chutney) and halal murtabak (paper-thin pancake stuffed with onion and seasoned meat, usually mutton).

Malaysian & Indonesian

Feast on Katong laksa (spicy coconut curry broth with noodles, prawns, cockles, fish cake, bean sprouts and laksa leaf), *ikan assam* (fried fish in a sour tamarind curry) and *nasi lemak* (coconut rice with fried fish and peanuts). Equally mouth-watering is *nasi padang*, which sees steamed rice paired with a choice of meat and vegetable dishes – simply pick and choose what you want and it's dolloped on a plate.

Peranakan

Peranakan (Nonya) food is a cross-cultural fusion of Chinese and Malay influences. Dishes are tangy, spicy and commonly flavoured with shallots, chillies, *belacan* (Malay fermented prawn paste), peanuts, preserved soya beans and galangal (a ginger-like root). Classics include *otak-otak,* a sausage-like blend of fish, coconut milk, chilli paste, galangal and herbs grilled in a banana leaf.

Tekka Centre

HAWKER $

18 🍴 MAP P64, A5

There's no shortage of subcontinental spice at this bustling hawker centre, wrapped around the sloshed guts and hacked bones of the wet market. Queue up for real-deal biryani, *dosa* (paper-thin lentil-flour pancake), *roti prata* (fried flatbread served with curry sauce) and *teh tarik* (sweet spiced Indian tea). Well worth seeking out is **Ah Rahman Royal Prata** (murtabak S$5-8; ⏱7am-10pm Tue-Sun), which flips some of Singapore's finest murtabak (stuffed savoury pancake). (cnr Serangoon & Buffalo Rds; dishes S$3-10; ⏱7am-11pm, stall hours vary; P🔗; MLittle India)

Piedra Negra

MEXICAN $$

19 🍴 MAP P64, F8

Sexy Latin beats, bombastic murals and tables right on free-spirited Haji Lane: this electric Mexican joint is a brilliant spot for cheapish cocktails and a little evening people-watching. Frozen or shaken, the margaritas pack a punch, and the joint's burritos, quesadillas, tacos and other Tex-Mex staples are filling and delish. (☎6291 1297; www.facebook.com/piedranegrasg; cnr Beach Rd & Haji Lane; mains S$10-22; ⏱noon-midnight Sun-Thu, to 2am Fri & Sat; 🛜; MBugis)

Meatsmith Little India

BARBECUE $$$

20 🍴 MAP P64, B5

Often referred to as the little cousin of Burnt Ends (p147) because it's partly owned by chef David Pynt, this American barbecue joint takes inspiration from the bustling streets of Little India that surround it. Think prime meats slathered in Indian spices and rubs then smoked, grilled or charred to perfection – the double-glazed beef rib is fall-off-the-bone tender. (☎9625 9056; www.meatsmith.com.sg; 21 Campbell Lane; mains S$16-48; ⏱5pm-midnight Tue-Fri, 11.30am-11.30pm Sat & Sun; MLittle India)

Komala Vilas

SOUTH INDIAN $

21 🍴 MAP P64, B4

This prime-position branch of the Komala Vilas chain is extremely popular because of the wallet-friendly, authentic dishes and generous portions. The wafer-thin *dosai* are legendary – order the meal and enjoy it served with three vegetable curries and condiments. Complete your feast with a warm masala tea, served in a traditional metal cup. (☎6293 6980; www.komala vilas.com.sg; 76-78 Serangoon Rd; dishes S$2.40-9; ⏱7am-10.30pm; 🔗; MLittle India)

Moghul Sweets

SWEETS $

If you're after a subcontinental sugar rush, tiny Moghul Sweets in the Little India Arcade (see 4 Map p64, B5) is the place to get it. Bite into luscious *gulab jamun* (syrup-soaked fried dough balls), harder-to-find *rasmalai* (paneer soaked in cardamom-infused clotted cream) and *barfi* (condensed milk and sugar slice) in flavours including pistachio, chocolate ... and carrot. (☑ 6392 5797; 01-16 Little India Arcade, 48 Serangoon Rd; sweets from S$1; ⏱ 9.30am-9.30pm; Ⓜ Little India)

Charlie's Peranakan

PERANAKAN $

22 ☒ MAP P64, F7

Charlie has garnered a loyal following over the past few decades for his comforting Nonya cuisine. After an eight-year hiatus he's back doing what he loves, and Singaporeans are joyous. Tucked away in the basement of Golden Mile Food Centre, you'll find a menu overflowing with Peranakan favourites – ask Charlie or his wife what they recommend and order that. (☑ 9789 6304; www.facebook.com/charliesperanakanfood;

New-School Hood

Once better known for hardware stores and boxing matches, Jalan Besar is metamorphosing into an area where heritage architecture meets new-school Singapore cool. It's a compact district, centred on Jln Besar and Tyrwhitt Rd. It's on the latter you'll find cult-status cafe-roaster **Chye Seng Huat Hardware** (CSHH Coffee Bar; Map p64, F2; ☑ 6396 0609; www.cshhcoffee.com; 150 Tyrwhitt Rd; ⏱ 9am-10pm Tue-Thu & Sun, to midnight Fri & Sat; Ⓜ Bendemeer, Farrer Park, Lavender).

Around the corner, on Horne Rd, is contemporary bakery-cafe **Two Bakers** (Map p64, F2; ☑ 6293 0329; www.two-bakers.com; 88 Horne Rd; pastries & cakes S$6.50-9; ⏱ 9am-6pm Mon, Wed, Thu & Sun, 10am-10pm Fri & Sat; Ⓜ Bendemeer, Lavender), where the sweet treats are created by Paris' Cordon Bleu-trained bakers. If it's late afternoon, cool down at nearby beer joint **Druggists** (Map p64, F2; ☑ 6341 5967; www.facebook.com/druggistssg; 119 Tyrwhitt Rd; ⏱ 4pm-midnight Mon-Thu, to 2am Fri & Sat, 2-10pm Sun; Ⓜ Bendemeer, Farrer Park, Lavender). Its 23 taps pour a rotating selection of craft brews from microbreweries around the world.

To reach Jalan Besar, alight at Bendermeer MRT and head to Lavender St; crossing this you'll find Tyrwhitt Rd on your left as you head north.

B1-30, Golden Mile Food Centre, 505 Beach Rd; dishes S$6-20; ⏱11.30am-7.30pm; Ⓜ Lavender, Nicoll Hwy, Bugis)

Hill Street Tai Hwa Pork Noodle
HAWKER $

23 ✴ MAP P64, F5

Locals have tried to keep this second-generation hawker stall – famous for Teochew-style bak chor mee (minced-pork noodles) – secret, but with its shiny Michelin star, that's now impossible. It's best to arrive early; before opening, you can grab a number instead of joining the forever-lengthening queue. Bowls come in four sizes; the S$8 option will fill you right up. (www.taihwa.com.sg; 01-12, Block 466, Crawford Lane; noodles S$6-10; ⏱9.30am-9pm; Ⓜ Lavender)

Beach Road Scissor Cut Curry Rice
HAWKER $

24 ✴ MAP P64, E3

The eponymous rice dish is possibly the most visually displeasing plate of food you'll ever see, but after one mouthful, you're bound to dive in for more. Choose from the items displayed in the glass cabinet and then watch the scissors snip it all into bite-sized pieces. Finally, curry and braised sauces are slopped on, and it's a gloriously delicious mess. (229 Jln Besar, cnr Kitchener Rd; dishes from $3.50; ⏱11am-3.30am; Ⓜ Lavender, Farrer Park)

Gandhi Restaurant
SOUTH INDIAN $

25 ✴ MAP P64, A4

It might be a canteen-style joint with erratic service and cheap decor, but who cares when the food is this good? Wash your hands by the sink at the back, and take a seat. A banana-leaf plate heaped with rice and condiments (set-meal thali) will appear; order extra items from the servers – chicken curry is a must – then tuck in. (29-31 Chander Rd; dishes S$2.50-6.50, set meals from S$4.50; ⏱11am-4pm & 6-11pm Mon-Fri, 11am-11pm Sat & Sun; Ⓜ Little India)

Nan Hwa Chong Fish-Head Steamboat Corner
CHINESE $$

26 ✴ MAP P64, F6

If you only try fish-head steamboat once, do it at this noisy, open-fronted veteran. Cooked on charcoal, the large pot of fish heads is brought to you in a steaming broth spiked with tee po (dried flat sole fish). One pot is enough for three or four people, and can stretch to more rice and side dishes. (☎6297 9319; www.facebook.com/nanhwachong; 812-816 North Bridge Rd; fish steamboats from S$20; ⏱4pm-1am; Ⓜ Bugis, Lavender)

Warong Nasi Pariaman
MALAYSIAN, INDONESIAN $

27 ✴ MAP P64, E6

This no-frills corner nasi padang (rice with curries) stall is the stuff of legend. Top choices include the delicate beef *rendang*, ayam bakar (grilled chicken with coconut sauce) and spicy sambal goreng (long beans, tempeh and fried beancurd). Get here by 11am to avoid the lunch hordes and by 5pm for the dinner queue. (☏6292 2374; www.pariaman.com.sg; 736-738 North Bridge Rd; dishes from S$3; ⏱7.30am-8pm; Ⓜ Bugis)

Zam Zam
MALAYSIAN $

28 ⊗ MAP P64, E7

These guys have been here since 1908, so they know what they're doing. Tenure hasn't bred complacency, though – the touts still try to herd customers in off the street, while frenetic chefs inside whip up delicious murtabak, the restaurant's speciality savoury pancakes, filled with succulent mutton, chicken, beef, venison or even sardines. Servings are epic, so order a medium between two. (☏6298 6320; www.zamzamsingapore.com; 697-699 North Bridge Rd; murtabak from S$5; ⏱7am-11pm; Ⓜ Bugis)

Drinking

Atlas
BAR

Straight out of 1920s Manhattan, this cocktail lounge in the lobby of the Parkview Museum (see 11 ◉ Map p64, E8) is an art-deco-inspired extravaganza, adorned with ornate bronze ceilings and low-lit plush lounge seating, with a drinks menu filled with decadent champagnes, curated cocktails and some mean martinis. However, it's the 12m-high gin wall, displaying over 1000

labels, that really makes a statement – make sure you ask for a tour.

Night-time bookings are essential, but if you arrive before 6pm you should still be able to nab a table. Doors open in the morning for coffees, and European–inspired bites are served throughout the day and well into the night. The afternoon tea (3pm to 5pm, from S$52) is also worth stopping in for. Dress to impress; no shorts or slippers after 5pm. (☏6396 4466; www.atlasbar.sg; Lobby, Parkview Sq, 600 North Bridge Rd; ⏱10am-1am Mon-Thu, to 2am Fri, 3pm-2am Sat; Ⓜ Bugis)

Maison Ikkoku The Art of Mixology
COCKTAIL BAR

29 ⊗ MAP P64, F7

Pimped with modern, industrial finishes and flushes of greenery, Maison Ikkoku The Art of Mixology is where real magic happens. There's no menu, so let the bartenders know what you like – a request for something sour might land you a tart, hot combo of spicy gin, grape, lemon and Japanese–chilli threads. Not cheap, but worth it. (☏6294 0078; www.ethanleslieleong.com; Level 2, 20 Kandahar St; ⏱bar 6pm-1am Sun-Thu, to 2am Fri & Sat; 🛜; Ⓜ Bugis)

Bar Stories
COCKTAIL BAR

30 ⊗ MAP P64, E7

This upstairs cocktail den is as small as it is hugely popular, so call ahead if heading in later in the week. If you're lucky you'll be sitting at the bar, where gung-ho barkeeps keep it freestyle, turning whatever spirit or flavour turns you on into a smashing libation. Creative, whimsical and often brilliant. (☑6298 0838; www.facebook.com/barstories.sg; 57A Haji Lane; ⏰5pm-1am Sun-Thu, to 2am Fri & Sat; Ⓜ Bugis)

Ginett
WINE BAR

31 🅟 MAP P64, A7

Pouring possibly the most affordable glass of wine in town (S$6), Ginett has garnered a large following of winer lovers who enjoy a decent glass of cheap French plonk. With soaring ceilings and a modern industrial bistro design, the space feels simultaneously sophisticated and casual. Take a seat

at the bar underneath row upon row of glistening hanging glasses, and sip the night away.

If you're feeling peckish, the cheese and cold cuts board will keep the hunger pangs at bay. (☑6809 7989; www.randblab.com; 200 Middle Rd; ⏰7am-11.30pm Sun-Thu, to 12.30am Fri & Sat; Ⓜ Bencoolen, Rochor)

Beast
BAR

32 🅟 MAP P64, F6

If you're after some hard liquor and only bourbon will do, pull up a stool at a rusty drum and start working your way through the Beast's grandiose selection, including home-brewed Southern Comfort. The kitchen churns out lip-smacking American

Little India & Kampong Glam Drinking

Zam Zam

HAFIZZUDDIN/SHUTTERSTOCK ©

Bollywood at the Rex

Where can you catch the Bollywood blockbusters advertised all over Little India? Why, at **Rex Cinemas** (Map p64, A5; ☑6337 6607; www.carnivalcinemas.sg; 2 Mackenzie Rd; tickets S$10; Ⓜ Little India), of course. This historic theatre screens films from around the subcontinent, most subtitled in English.

Deep South–style food; the fried chicken and waffles is a standout. Live-music lovers shouldn't miss Thursday's open-mike night. (☑6295 0017; www.thebeast.sg; 17 Jln Klapa; ☺5pm-midnight Mon-Wed, to 1am Thu & Fri, 11am-midnight Sat & Sun; Ⓜ Bugis)

Prince of Wales   PUB

33 MAP P64, B5

The closest thing to a pub in Little India, this grungy Aussie hangout is an affable, popular spot, with a small beer garden, a pool table and sports screens. Weekly staples include Wednesday quiz night (from 8pm) and live music every other night of the week. There are plenty of good drink deals to keep the good times rolling. (☑6299 0130; www.pow.com.sg; 101 Dunlop St; ☺5pm-1am Mon-Thu, 3pm-2am Fri & Sat, to 1am Sun; Ⓜ Rochor, Jalan Besar)

Entertainment

Singapore Dance Theatre   DANCE

34 🟢 MAP P64, C8

This is the headquarters of Singapore's premier dance company, which keeps fans swooning with its repertoire of classic ballets and contemporary works, many of which are performed at Esplanade – Theatres on the Bay (p49). The true highlight is the group's Ballet under the Stars season at **Fort Canning Park** (☑1800 471 7300; www.nparks.gov.sg; bounded by Hill St, Canning Rise, Clemenceau Ave & River Valley Rd; Ⓜ Dhoby Ghaut, Clarke Quay, Fort Canning), which usually runs midyear. See the website for program details. (☑6338 0611; www.singaporedancetheatre.com; 07-02/03, Bugis+, 201 Victoria St; Ⓜ Bugis)

BluJaz Café   LIVE MUSIC

35 🟢 MAP P64, E7

Bohemian pub BluJaz is one of the best options in town for live music, with regular jazz jams, and other acts playing anything from blues to rockabilly. Check the website for events, which includes DJ-spun funk, R&B and retro nights, as well as 'Talk Cock' open-mike comedy nights on Wednesdays and Thursdays. Cover charge for some shows. (☑6292 3800; www.blujazcafe.net; 11 Bali Lane; ☺9am-12.30am Mon-Tue, to 1am Wed-Thu, to 2.30am Fri-Sat, noon-midnight Sun; 🛜; Ⓜ Bugis)

Going Om
LIVE MUSIC

36 ⭐ MAP P64, E7

Right on Haji Lane, Going Om is a raffish, free-spirited cafe with nightly live music. It's an atmospheric spot, with candlelit tables, smooth acoustic sets (mostly well-executed covers) and no shortage of carefree punters dancing in the laneway. The boho spirit extends to the beverage list, which includes 'chakra' drinks of seven colours (one for each chakra, dude). (📞6396 3592; www.going-om.com.sg; 63 Haji Lane; 🕑noon-midnight Sun-Thu, to 1am Fri & Sat; Ⓜ Bugis)

Wild Rice
THEATRE

37 ⭐ MAP P64, A4

Singapore's sexiest theatre group is based in Kerbau Rd but performs shows elsewhere in the city (as well as abroad). A mix of home-grown and foreign works, productions range from farce to serious politics, fearlessly wading into issues not commonly on the agenda in Singapore.

Many performances take place at the LASALLE College of the Arts, located at 1 McNally St, just steps from the Rochor MRT station. (📞6292 2695; www.wildrice.com.sg; 65 Kerbau Rd; Ⓜ Little India)

Hood
LIVE MUSIC

38 ⭐ MAP P64, C8

Inside the Bugis+ mall, Hood's street-art interior sets a youthful scene for nightly music jams with acts such as Rush Hour and Singapore Char Siew Baos. If it's undiscovered talent you're after, head in for the weekly 'Saturday Original Session', a showcase for budding musos itching to share their singer-songwriter skills. (📞6221 8846; www.hoodbarandcafe.com; 05-07 Bugis+, 201 Victoria St; 🕑5pm-1am Sun-Thu, to 3am Fri & Sat; Ⓜ Bugis)

Shopping

Sifr Aromatics
PERFUME

39 🅐 MAP P64, F7

This Zen-like perfume laboratory belongs to third-generation perfumer Johari Kazura, whose exquisite creations include the heady East (30mL S$125), a blend of oud, rose absolute, amber and neroli. The focus is on custom-made fragrances (consider calling ahead to arrange an appointment), with other heavenly offerings including affordable, high-quality body balms, scented candles and vintage perfume bottles. (📞6392 1966; www.sifr.sg; 42 Arab St; 🕑11am-8pm Mon-Sat, to 5pm Sun; Ⓜ Bugis)

Supermama
GIFTS & SOUVENIRS

40 🅐 MAP P64, F8

Tucked around the corner from Arab St, this gallery-esque store is a treasure trove of contemporary giftware. Circle the huge central bench while you pore over the Singapore-inspired wares, most created by local designers. The

Instagram Paradise

Narrow, pastel-hued **Haji Lane** (Map p106, E8; M Bugis) harbours a handful of quirky boutiques and plenty of colourful street art. Shops turn over fast due to exorbitant rents, however a long-term favourite is concept store Mondays Off, which stocks everything from contemporary local ceramics to art mags and geometric racks to store them on. For a sweet treat, stop off at whimsical Windowsill Pies.

blue-and-white fine-porcelain dishes, made in Japan, are the headliners. (☎6291 1946; www. supermama.sg; 265 Beach Rd; ⏱11am-8pm; M Bugis)

Mustafa Centre DEPARTMENT STORE

41 🔒 MAP P64, C2

Little India's bustling Mustafa Centre is a magnet for budget shoppers, most of them from the subcontinent. It's a sprawl-ing place, selling everything from electronics and garish gold jewellery to shoes, bags, luggage and beauty products. There's also a large supermarket with a great range of Indian foodstuffs. If you can't handle crowds, avoid the place on Sundays. (☎6295 5855; www.mustafa.com.sg; 145 Syed Alwi Rd; ⏱24hr; M Farrer Park)

Rugged Gentlemen Shoppe FASHION & ACCESSORIES

42 🔒 MAP P64, B5

A vintage-inspired ode to American working-class culture, this little menswear store offers a clued-in selection of rugged threads and accessories, including Red Wing boots, grooming products and made-in-house leather goods. Stock up on plaid shirts, sweat tops and harder-to-find denim from brands like Japan's Iron Heart and China's Red Cloud. (☎6396 4568; www.uggedgentlemenshoppe.com; 8 Perak Rd; ⏱noon-8pm Mon-Sat, by ap-pointment Sun; M Rochor, Jalan Besar)

Bugis Street Market MARKET

43 🔒 MAP P64, C7

What was once Singapore's most infamous sleaze pit – packed with foreign servicemen on R&R and gambling dens – is now its most famous undercover street market, crammed with cheap clothes, shoes, accessories and manicurists. It's especially popular with teens and twenty-somethings – in a nod to its past, there's even a sex shop. (☎6338 9513; www.bugisstreet.com.sg; 3 New Bugis St; ⏱11am-10pm; M Bugis)

Little Shophouse ARTS & CRAFTS

44 🔒 MAP P64, F7

Traditional Peranakan beadwork is a dying art, but it's kept very much alive in this shop and workshop. The shop's colourful slippers are designed by craftsman Robert Sng and hand-beaded by himself and

TKKURIKAWA/GETTY IMAGES ©

Haji Lane

his sister, Irene. While they're not cheap (approximately S$1000), each pair takes a painstaking 100 hours to complete. You'll also find Peranakan-style tea sets, crockery, vases, handbags and jewellery. (📞6295 2328; 43 Bussorah St; ⏰10am-5pm; Ⓜ Bugis)

Sim Lim Square ELECTRONICS

45 🅐 MAP P64, B6

A byword for all that is cut price and geeky, Sim Lim Square is jammed with stalls selling soundcards cameras, laptops and games consoles. If you know what you're doing, there are deals to be had, but the untutored are likely to be out of their depth. Bargain hard (but politely) and always check that the warranty is valid in your home country. (📞6338 3859; www.simlimsquare.com.sg; 1 Rochor Canal Rd; ⏰10.30am-9pm; Ⓜ Rochor, Jalan Besar)

Explore ✪
Orchard Road

What was once a dusty road lined with spice plantations and orchards is now a 2.5km torrent of magnificent malls, department stores and speciality shops. Indeed, you can shop until you drop, pick yourself up and continue spending. But wait there's more, including drool-inducing food courts and a heritage-listed side street rocking with bars and happy-hour specials.

The Short List

○ **ION Orchard Mall (p93)** *Shopping at Singapore's sleekest mall.*

○ **Tanglin Shopping Centre (p93)** *Hunting for antique treasures.*

○ **Emerald Hill Road (p86)** *Strolling this heritage-packed area.*

○ **Iggy's (p87)** *Tasting creative fusion dishes.*

○ **Killiney Kopitiam (p89)** *Enjoying breakfast at the original locals' coffeeshop.*

Getting There & Around

Ⓜ Orchard Rd is served by no less than three MRT stations: Orchard, Somerset and Dhoby Ghaut, so there's really no need to use any other form of transport.

Neighbourhood Map on p84

Orchard Road KOMAR/SHUTTERSTOCK ©

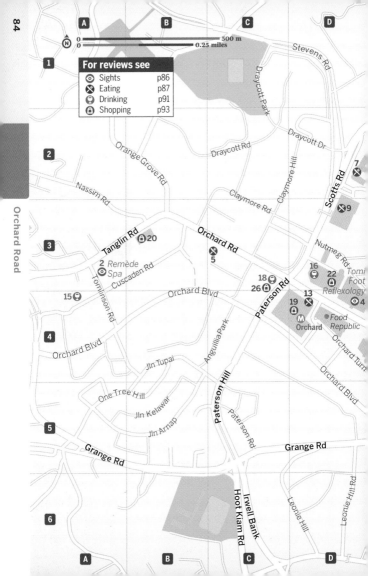

For reviews see

⊙	Sights	p86
✗	Eating	p87
⊜	Drinking	p91
⊕	Shopping	p93

0   500 m
0   0.25 miles

Stevens Rd

Draycott Park

Draycott Rd

Draycott Dr

Orange Grove Rd

Claymore Hill

Claymore Rd

Scotts Rd

✗7

✗9

Nassim Rd

Orchard Rd

Nutmeg Rd

Tanglin Rd   ⊕20

✗5

16 ⊕   22 ⊕

Tomi
Foot
Reflexology

2 Remède
⊙ Spa

Cuscaden Rd

Orchard Blvd

18 ⊕
26 ⊕

Paterson Rd

13

⊙4

15 ⊜

Tomlinson Rd

19 ⊕   ✗

Anguillia Park

Ⓜ Orchard

● Food
Republic

Orchard Blvd

Orchard Turn

Jln Tupai

Orchard Blvd

One Tree Hill

Jln Kelawar

Paterson Hill

Jln Arnap

Paterson Rd

Grange Rd

Grange Rd

Irwell Bank

Hoot Kiam Rd

Leonie Hill

Leonie Hill Rd

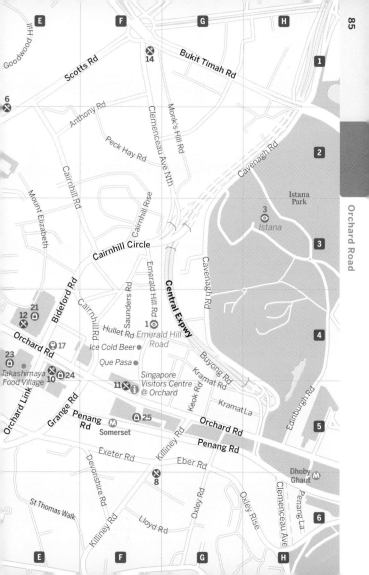

Sights

Emerald Hill Road ARCHITECTURE

1 ◉ MAP P84, F4

Take time out from your shopping to wander up frangipani-scented Emerald Hill Rd, graced with some of Singapore's finest terrace houses. Special mentions go to No 56 (one of the earliest buildings from 1902), Nos 39 to 45 (unusually wide frontages and a grand Chinese–style entrance gate), and Nos 120 to 130 (art-deco features dating from around 1925). At the Orchard Rd, there is a cluster of popular bars housed in fetching shophouse renovations. (Emerald Hill Rd; Ⓜ Somerset)

Remède Spa SPA

2 ◉ MAP P84, A3

Reputed to have the best massage therapists in town, the St Regis Hotel's in-house spa is also home to the award-winning Pedi:Mani:Cure Studio by renowned pedicurist Bastien Gonzalez. Remède's wet lounge – a marbled wonderland of steam room, sauna, ice fountains and spa baths – is a perfect prelude to standout treatments like the warm jade-stone massage ($300). (☎ 6506 6896; www.remedespasing apore.com; St Regis Hotel, 29 Tanglin Rd; massage from S$105; ⏰ 9am-11pm; Ⓜ Orchard)

Istana PALACE

3 ◉ MAP P84, H3

The grand, whitewashed, neo-classical home of Singapore's president, set in 16 hectares of grounds, was built by the British between 1867 and 1869 as Government House, and is open to visitors just five times a year. Check the website to confirm exact dates. Only on these days will you get the chance to stroll past the nine-hole golf course, through the beautiful terraced gardens and into some of the reception rooms. Bring your passport and get here early; queues build quickly.

The rest of the time you can visit the **Istana Heritage Gallery** (☎ 6904 4289; www.istana.gov. sg; admission free; ⏰ 10am-6pm, closed Wed) across Orchard Rd or glance through the heavily guarded gates. (www.istana.gov.sg; Orchard Rd; grounds/palace S$2/4; ⏰ 8.30am-6pm Chinese New Year, Labour Day, National Day, Diwali & Hari Raya Puasa/Eid-ul Fitr; Ⓜ Dhoby Ghaut)

Tomi Foot Reflexology MASSAGE

4 ◉ MAP P84, D4

A no-frills massage joint lurking in the 1970s throwback Lucky Plaza. Head in for one of the best rubdowns in town, provided by the tactile team in matching pink polos. Techniques include acupressure and shiatsu, all approved by Jesus and Mary, hanging on the wall. (☎ 6736 4249; 01-94 Lucky Plaza, 304 Orchard Rd; 30min reflexology/massage S$30/50; ⏰ 10am-10pm; Ⓜ Orchard)

Eating

Iggy's

FUSION $$$

5 MAP P84, C3

Iggy's refined, sleek design promises something special, and with a large picture window drawing your eye to the magic happening in the kitchen, you can take a peek. Head chef Aitor Jeronimo Orive delivers with his ever-changing, highly seasonal, creative fusion dishes. Superlatives extend to the wine list, one of the city's finest. (6732 2234; www.iggys.com.sg; Level 3, Hilton Hotel, 581 Orchard Rd; set lunch/dinner from S$85/195; 7-9.30pm, plus noon-1.30pm Thu-Sat; ; Orchard)

Buona Terra

ITALIAN $$$

6 MAP P84, E2

This intimate, linen-lined Italian restaurant is one of Singapore's unsung glories. In the kitchen is young Lombard chef Denis Lucchi, who turns exceptional ingredients into elegant, modern dishes, like seared duck liver with poached peach, amaretti crumble and Vin Santo ice cream. Lucchi's right-hand man is Emilian sommelier Gabriele Rizzardi, whose wine list, though expensive, is extraordinary. (6733 0209; www.buonaterra.com.sg; 29 Scotts Rd; 3-/5-course lunch S$48/128, 4-/6-course dinner S$128/168; noon-2.30pm & 6.30-10.30pm Mon-Fri, 6.30-10.30pm Sat; ; Newton)

Emerald Hill Rd

Black & Whites

Often seen peeking through the lush, forested corners of Singapore, these distinctive black-and-white bungalows are a reminder of Singapore's colonial past. Usually built by wealthy plantation owners between the late 19th century and WWII, these grand homes have retained the character and charm of days gone by. The design itself was greatly influenced by the Arts and Craft movement that originated in England in the 1860s and renewed value on craftsmanship, – a counter reaction to England's rapid industrialisation.

Once there were 10,000 of these beauties in Singapore, but after being left derelict post-WWII, approximately only 500 remain. The majority are now owned by the government and are regarded as National Monuments; however, some are rented to families and businesses. While they are incredibly popular with the expat community for their large gardens and airy interiors (rare to find in space-constrained Singapore), rental costs are hefty and hopeful tenants must bid to secure two-year leases.

Some Black & Whites are occasionally opened to the public, but the easiest way to see inside one is to join a tour with **Jane's SG Tours** (www.janestours.sg; group tours S$50-90), but be sure to book in advance. Alternatively, a number of restaurants call these properties home – you'll find several along Scotts Rd. If you're in the mood for a fancy Italian dinner, our pick is Buona Terra (p87).

Paradise Dynasty   CHINESE $$

Preened staffers in headsets whisk you into this svelte dumpling den inside the ION mall (see 19 🔒 Map p84, D4), passing a glassed-in kitchen where Chinese chefs stretch their noodles and steam their buns. Skip the novelty-flavoured *xiao long bao* (soup dumplings) for the original version, which arguably beat those of legendary competitor Din Tai Fung (p93). Beyond these, standouts include *la mian* (hand-pulled noodles) with buttery, braised pork belly. No reservations taken. (www.paradisegroup.com.sg; 04-12A ION Orchard, 2 Orchard Turn; dishes S$5-20; ⊙11am-9.30pm, from 10.30am Sat & Sun; MOrchard)

Gordon Grill   INTERNATIONAL $$$

7 MAP P84, D2

With its old-world charm – complete with crisp linens – and its famed steaks, Gordon Grill, housed inside a colonial-era hotel, is a step back in time compared with ultramodern Orchard Rd. It's as much an experience as it is a meal, so this is perhaps the best place for splashing out on the wagyu beef, ordered by weight, cut at your table and cooked to your specifications. (☎6730 1744; www.goodwoodparkhotel.com; Goodwood Park Hotel, 22 Scotts Rd; mains S$44-62; ⏰noon-2.30pm & 7-10.30pm; 🛜; Ⓜ Orchard)

Killiney Kopitiam CAFE $

8 MAP P84, F6

Start the day the old-school way at this veteran coffee joint, adorned with endearingly lame laminated jokes. Order a strong *kopi* (coffee), a serve of *kaya* (coconut jam) toast and a side of soft-boiled egg. Crack open the egg, add a dash of soy sauce and white pepper, then dip your *kaya* toast in it. (☎6734 3910; www.killiney-kopitiam.com; 67 Killiney Rd; dishes S$1-7; ⏰6am-11pm, to 6pm Tue & Sun; Ⓜ Somerset)

Wasabi Tei JAPANESE $$

9 MAP P84, D3

Channelling 1972 with its Laminex countertop and wood-panelled walls, this tiny, cash-only sushi bar feels like a scrumptious local secret. Nab a spot at the counter and watch the masterful chef make raw fish sing with flavour. Note: the newer sibling restaurant next door is no substitute for the original. No reservations so make sure to arrive before the lunchtime rush. (05-70 Far East Plaza, 14 Scotts Rd; mains S$10-35; ⏰noon-3pm & 5.30-9.30pm Mon-Sat; Ⓜ Orchard)

Providore CAFE $$

10 MAP P84, E4

Waiting at the top of Mandarin Gallery's outdoor escalator is Providore, a cool, upbeat cafe with white tiles, industrial details and shelves neatly stocked with gourmet pantry fillers. Sip a full-bodied latte or scan the menu for an all-bases list of options, from breakfast-friendly organic muesli and pancakes, to gourmet salads and sandwiches, to a carbalicious lobster mac and cheese. Weekend brunch is especially popular, so make sure you head in before 11am. (☎6732 1565; www.theprovidore.com; 02-05 Mandarin Gallery, 333A Orchard Rd; dishes S$12-29; ⏰9am-10pm; 🛜; Ⓜ Somerset)

Signs A Taste Of Vietnam Pho VIETNAMESE $

11 MAP P84, F5

Bowls of flavoursome broth and Vietnamese spring rolls bursting with freshness are the signature dishes at this no-frills eatery, and it's the owners, deaf couple Anthony and Angela, will be dishing up the goods. Enter with a smile and Anthony will quickly have you ticking boxes on the menu. Portions are generous. (B1-07 Midpoint Orchard, 220 Orchard Rd; dishes S$5-8; ⏰11am-9pm; Ⓜ Somerset)

Food Court Favourites

Burrow into the basement of most malls on Orchard Rd and you'll find a food court with stall upon stall selling cheap, freshly cooked dishes from all over the world. One of the best is heaving **Takashimaya Food Village** (Map p84, E4; 6506 0458; www.takashimaya. com.sg; B2 Takashimaya Department Store, Ngee Ann City, 391 Orchard Rd; dishes S$4-17; 10am-9.30pm; ; Orchard), which serves up a *Who's Who* of Japanese, Korean and other Asian culinary classics. Another top spot is **Food Republic** (Map p84, D4; www.foodrepublic. com.sg; Level 4, Wisma Atria, 435 Orchard Rd; dishes S$5-15; 10am-10pm; ; Orchard); OK, so this one is not actually in the basement, but the formula remains the same – lip-smacking food, a plethora of choices and democratic prices. The roving 'aunties' pushing around trolleys filled with drinks and dim sum complete the experience.

Tambuah Mas INDONESIAN $$

12 MAP P84, E4

Hiding shyly in a corner of Paragon's food-packed basement, Tambuah Mas is where Indonesian expats head for a taste of home. Bright, modern and good value for Orchard Rd, it proudly makes much of what it serves from scratch, a fact evident in what could possibly be Singapore's best beef *rendang*. No reservations, so arrive early if dining Thursday to Saturday. (6733 2220; www. tambuahmas.com.sg; B1-44 Paragon, 290 Orchard Rd; mains S$8-29; 11am-10pm; ; Somerset)

Ice Cream Stand ICE CREAM $

13 MAP P84, D4

Against the shiny new facades of Orchard Rd's high-end malls, you'll spot a few out-of-place-looking, weather-beaten beach umbrellas.

Underneath each one of them, a favourite Singaporean snack (ice-cream sandwiches) are created. Pick your flavour and watch as a chunk is carved off the slab and popped between either two wafers or a slice of soft, rainbow bread. (Orchard Rd; S$1-1.50; 9am-9pm; Orchard, Somerset)

Newton Food Centre HAWKER $

14 MAP P84, F1

Opened in 1971 this famous hawker centre still has a great, at times smoky, atmosphere. You could eat here for a whole year and never get bored. Well-known stalls include Alliance seafood (01-27), Hup Kee fried oyster omelette (01-73) and Kwee Heng (01-13). Touts can be a problem for foreigners, but ignore them. The best stalls don't need to tout. (500 Clemenceau Ave Nth; dishes from S$2; noon-2am; Newton)

Drinking

Manhattan

BAR

15 🚇 MAP P84, A4

Step back in time to the golden age of fine drinking at this handsome *Mad Men*–esque bar, where long-forgotten cocktails come back to life. Grouped by eras of New York, the drinks menu is ever-changing; however, waistcoated bartenders are only too happy to guide you. Sunday brings freshly shucked oysters, and an adults-only cocktail brunch (S$150) with make-your-own bloody Marys. Number 1 on Asia's 50 Best Bars 2017–18 list, this is not one to miss. (📞6725 3377; www.regenthotels.com/Singapore; Level 2, Regent, 1 Cuscaden Rd; ⏰5pm-1am, to 2am Fri & Sat, noon-3pm Sun; Ⓜ Orchard)

Other Room

BAR

16 🚇 MAP P84, D3

You'll find this hidden drinking house, a throwback to a bygone era, behind a secret door in the Singapore Marriott lobby – ring the doorbell for entry. Peruse the 50-page drinks menu and settle in for a night to remember. Award-winning mixologist Dario Knox takes spirits seriously; the American oak-barrel-aged spirits in different finishings are where you should begin. Night owls will rejoice at the late closing time by Singapore standards. (📞6100 7778; www.theotherroom.com.sg; 01-05 Singapore Marriott, 320 Orchard Rd; ⏰6pm-3am, to 4am Fri-Sun; Ⓜ Orchard)

Newton Food Centre

Back-Alley Bars

It might not be a back alley as such, but Emerald Hill Rd feels like miles away from the frenetic energy of nearby Orchard Rd. Its cluster of bars – housed in century-old Peranakan shophouses – are popular with the after-work crowd. Top billing goes to neon-pimped **Ice Cold Beer** (Map p84, F4; 6735 9929; www.ice-cold-beer.com; 9 Emerald Hill Rd; 5pm-2am, from 2pm Sat & Sun; MSomerset), a boozy bar with dart boards, pool table, tongue-in-cheek soft-core wall pin-ups and daily happy-hour deals from 5pm to 9pm. For a slightly classier evening, head to **Que Pasa** (Map p84, F4; 6235 6626; www.quepasa.com.sg; 7 Emerald Hill Rd; 1.30pm-2am, from 5.30pm Sun; MSomerset), where you can work your way through the extensive wine list.

TWG Tea
TEAHOUSE

Posh tea purveyor TWG inside the ION mall (see 19 Map p84, D4) sells more than 800 single-estate teas and blends from around the world, from English breakfast to Rolls–Royce varieties like 24-car-at-gold-coated Grand Golden Yin Zhen. Edibles include tea-infused macarons (the *bain de roses* is divine), ice cream and sorbet. Also available is an all-day dining menu. (6735 1837; www.twgtea.com; 02-21 ION Orchard, 2 Orchard Rd; 10am-10pm; ; MOrchard)

Bar Canary
BAR

17 MAP P84, E4

Canary-yellow sofas, artificial turf and the sound of humming traffic and screeching birds – this alfresco bar hovers high above frenetic Orchard Rd. It's fab for an evening tipple, with well-positioned fans. Book at least a week ahead for its Wednesday Girls' Night Out: S$55, plus tax, for free-flow champagne, house pours and selected cocktails from 7pm to 9pm. (6603 8855; www.parkhotelgroup.com/orchard; Level 4, Park Hotel Orchard, 270 Orchard Rd, entry on Bideford Rd; noon-1am, to 2am Fri & Sat; ; MSomerset)

Privé
CAFE

18 MAP P84, C3

With its pedestrian pavement location and terraced seating, this Parisian–style cafe is the perfect ringside spot to watch the masses strutting up and down Orchard Rd. Serving decent cafe fare, plus soups, pastas and all-day breakfasts, Privé has a good cocktail and wine list and more than 15 whiskies. Happy hour is 5pm to 8pm; book for the best seats. (6776 0777; www.theprivegroup.com.sg; 01-K1 Wheelock Place, 501 Orchard Rd; 9am-1am; MOrchard)

Shopping

ION Orchard Mall

MALL

19 🔒 MAP P84, D4

Rising directly above Orchard MRT station, futuristic ION is the cream of Orchard Rd malls. Basement floors focus on mere-mortal high-street labels like Zara and Uniqlo, while upper-floor tenants read like the index of *Vogue*. Dining options range from food-court bites to posher nosh, and the attached 56-storey tower, **ION Sky** (admission free; ⏱2-8.30pm) has a top-floor viewing gallery. (📞6238 8228; www.ionorchard.com; 2 Orchard Turn; ⏱10am-10pm; 📶; Ⓜ Orchard)

Tanglin Shopping Centre

MALL

20 🔒 MAP P84, B3

This retro mall specialises in Asian art and is the place to come for quality rugs, carvings, ornaments, jewellery, paintings, furniture and the like. Top billing goes to **Antiques of the Orient** (📞6734 9351; www.aoto.com.sg; ⏱10am-5.30pm Mon-Sat, 11am-3.30pm Sun), with original and reproduction prints, photographs, and maps of Singapore and Asia. Especially beautiful are the richly coloured botanical drawings commissioned by British colonist William Farquhar. (📞6737 0849; www.tanglinsc.com; 19 Tanglin Rd; ⏱10am-10pm; Ⓜ Orchard)

Paragon

MALL

21 🔒 MAP P84, E4

Even if you don't have a Black Amex, strike a pose inside this Maserati of Orchard Rd malls. Status labels include Burberry, Prada, Jimmy Choo and Gucci. High-street brands include Ted Baker and G-Star Raw. In the basement you'll find dumpling king **Din Tai Fung** (📞6836 8336; www.dintaifung.com.sg; buns S$2, dumplings S$5-16; ⏱11am-10pm, from 10am Sat & Sun) and a large Cold Storage supermarket. (📞6738 5535; www.paragon.com.sg; 290 Orchard Rd; ⏱10am-10pm; 📶; Ⓜ Somerset)

Tangs

DEPARTMENT STORE

22 🔒 MAP P84, D3

Since opening its doors more than 85 years ago, Tangs has become a Singaporean institution. This five-floor department store is popular with all generations, selling business suits, formal evening attire and streetwear in the huge clothes section, as well as electronics, shoes and some of the best homewares in town. (📞6737 5500; www.tangs.com; 310 Orchard Rd; ⏱10.30am-9.30pm, to 8.30pm Sun; 📶; Ⓜ Orchard)

Ngee Ann City

MALL

23 🔒 MAP P84, E4

It might look like a forbidding mausoleum, but this marble-and-granite behemoth promises retail giddiness on its seven floors. International luxury brands compete for space with sprawling bookworm nirvana **Kinokuniya** (☎ 6737 5021; www.kinokuniya.com. sg; ⏱ 10am-9.30pm) and up-market Japanese department store **Takashimaya** (☎ 6738 1111; www. takashimaya.com.sg; ⏱ 10am-9.30pm; 🛜), home to Takashimaya Food Village (p90), one of the strip's best food courts. (☎ 6506 0461; www.ngeeanncity.com.sg; 391 Orchard Rd; ⏱ 10am-9.30pm; Ⓜ Somerset)

Beyond the Vines   CLOTHING

24 🔒 MAP P84, E4

Singaporean womenswear label Beyond the Vines offers functional and luxurious basics in soothing, pastel hues. Browse the modern brass racks that surround the central ottoman, complete with a real tree in the middle, and be surprised by the very reasonable price tags on these mix-and-match separates in fabrics such as jersey, cotton and silk blends. (☎ 8157 0577; www.beyondthevines.com; 02-21 Mandarin Gallery, 333A Orchard Rd; ⏱ 10am-9pm; Ⓜ Somerset)

In Good Company   CLOTHING

One of Singapore's most lauded home-grown fashion labels has experienced a spectacular rise, just three years since the design house opened its flagship store in Orchard Rd's swanky ION mall (see **19** 🔒 Map p84, D4)). All-white interiors with industrial black racks, light woods, granite and polished concrete create a serene canvas to display the label's geo-metric modern aesthetic that also includes lust-worthy statement necklaces.

Wheelock Place

Hidden in the back is an outpost of the Plain Vanilla Bakery (p159), a heaven for cupcake lovers. (📞6509 4786; www.ingoodcompany. asia; B1-06 ION Orchard, 2 Orchard Turn; 🕐10am-9.30pm; Ⓜ Orchard)

Orchardgateway

MALL

25 🅰 MAP P84, F5

Occupying a position on both sides of Orchard Rd, conveniently linked by an underground and above-ground walkway, this mall is home to boundary-pushing fashion stores **Sects Shop** (📞9889 2179; www. sectsshop.com; 🕐noon-10pm) and **i.t** (📞6702 7186; www.itlabels.com.sg; 🕐11am-9pm, to 10pm Fri & Sat).

Head to level four, for unique fashion and accessories tailored to discerning gentlemen. (📞6513 4633; www.orchardgateway.sg; 277 & 218 Orchard Rd; 🕐10.30am-10.30pm; Ⓜ Somerset)

Wheelock Place

MALL

26 🅰 MAP P84, C3

Linked to ION Orchard and the MRT by an underground walkway, Wheelock Place is more than just spas and laser clinics. Dapper gents

Orchard Rd's Last Building Block

With new shopping malls being shoehorned into every available space on Orchard Rd, why, many visitors ask, does the Thai embassy occupy such large, prominent grounds in an area of staggeringly expensive real estate? Back in the 1990s the Thai government was reportedly offered S$139 million for the site, but they turned it down because selling the land, bought by Thailand for S$9000 in 1983 by the revered King Chulalongkorn (Rama V), would be seen as an affront to his memory. And so, it remains, coveted by frustrated developers.

head to Benjamin Barker for sharp shirts, suits and accessories, while **Threadbare & Squirrel** (📞6235 0680; www.threadbareandsquirrel.com; 🕐10.30am-9.30pm) is known for quirky accessories, individualistic threads and artisan jewellery. (www. wheelockplace.com; 501 Orchard Rd; 🕐10am-10pm; Ⓜ Orchard)

Worth a Trip 🔭
Singapore Zoo

Singapore Zoo is a verdant, tropical wonderland of spacious, naturalistic enclosures, freely roaming animals and interactive attractions. Breakfast with orang-utans, dodge flying foxes, mosey up to tree-hugging sloths, even snoop around a replica African village. Then there's the setting: 26 soothing hectares on a lush peninsula jutting out onto the waters of the Upper Seletar Reservoir. It's a Singapore must-do.

📞 6269 3411

www.wrs.com.sg

80 Mandai Lake Rd

adult/child under 13yr/3yr S$33/22/free

🕐 8.30am-6pm

🚻

Jungle Breakfast with Wildlife

Orang-utans are the zoo's celebrity residents and you can devour a scrumptious breakfast buffet in their company at **Jungle Breakfast with Wildlife** (Ah Meng Restaurant; adult/child under 12yr/6yr S$35/25/free; ☺9-10.30am). If you miss out, get your photo taken with them at the neighbouring Free Ranging Orang-utan Island (11am, 3.30pm and 4.30pm). Best of all, you're free to use your own camera.

Fragile Forest

Close encounters await at the Fragile Forest, a giant biodome that replicates the stratas of a rainforest. Cross paths with free-roaming butterflies and colourful lories, swooping Malayan flying foxes and unperturbed ring-tailed lemurs. The pathway leads up to the forest canopy and the dome's most chilled-out locals, the two-toed sloths.

Great Rift Valley of Ethiopia

Featuring cliffs, a waterfall and a stream fashioned to look like the Ethiopian hinterland, the evocative Great Rift Valley exhibit is home to Hamadryas baboons, Nubian ibexes, banded mongooses, black-backed jackals and rock hyraxes. You'll also find replica Ethiopian villages, complete with dwelling huts and an insight into the area's harsh living conditions.

Rainforest Kidzworld

Let your own little critters go wild at **Rainforest Kidzworld** (carousel/pony rides per person S$4/6; ☺9am-6pm; 🚌138), a Technicolor play area complete with slides, swings and a carousel. Kids can also ride ponies, feed farmyard animals and squeal to their heart's content in the wet-play area. Swimwear is available for purchase if you haven't brought your own.

★ **Top Tips**

○ Try to arrive as the gates open (8.30am) – not only is it cooler for you, but the animals tend to be more active in the early morning.

○ Consider combining your trip with a visit to the neighbouring Night Safari (p98).

○ Feeding times are staggered. Check the website for details.

○ Tickets bought online receive a 5% discount. If you're planning on visiting Singapore Zoo, Night Safari, River Safari or Jurong Bird Park, check out the combined park tickets and save up to 50%.

✗ **Take a Break**

There's no shortage of eateries on-site, serving everything from American fast food to local staples.

★ **Getting There**

Catch the train to Ang Mo Kio MRT and then bus 138. It will cost about S$25 for a taxi from the CBD.

Worth a Trip 🔭
Night Safari

Singapore's acclaimed Night Safari offers a different type of nightlife. Home to over 130 species of animals, the park's barriers seem to melt away in the darkness, giving you the feeling of being up close with the likes of lions, leopards and elephants. The atmosphere is heightened by strolling antelopes, often passing within inches of the trams you're travelling in.

📞 6269 3411

www.wrs.com.sg

80 Mandai Lake Rd

adult/child under 13yr/3yr
S$47/31/free

🕘 7.15pm-midnight

👫

Electric Tram Tour

Almost everyone heads to the tram queue as they enter, and you should too. These near-silent, open-sided vehicles come with a guide whose commentary is a good introduction to the park's animals and different habitats. The journey lasts 45 minutes, though we highly recommend that you alight at the designated stops to explore more of the park on foot. If possible, opt for the second or third cars as they offer the best views.

Walking Trails

The grounds offer four interlinked walking trails, each taking between 20 and 30 minutes to explore. Get centimetres away from wild spotted felines on the Leopard Trail, also home to the thrilling Giant Flying Squirrel aviary. Peer at splash-happy cats and the world's largest bat, the Malayan flying fox, on the Fishing Cat Trail. The Wallaby Trail is home to a walk-through wallaby habitat, while the outstanding East Lodge Trail awaits with highly endangered babirusas and elegant Malayan tigers. Make sure you wear comfortable shoes and bring insect repellent and an umbrella, just in case.

Creatures of the Night

If you have kids in tow, consider checking out **Creatures of the Night** (⏲7.15pm, 8.30pm, 9.30pm, plus 10.30pm Fri & Sat), an interactive 25-minute show with stars that include binturongs, civets and a hyena. Seating is unassigned, so it's a good idea to arrive a little early to secure a good vantage point. Shows may be cancelled in case of wet weather.

We must note that animal performances have been criticised by animal-welfare groups, who say that captivity is debilitating and stressful for animals, and that this is exacerbated by human interaction.

★ **Top Tips**

○ When returning from the safari, catch a bus at around 10.45pm as the last MRT train leaves Ang Mo Kio at 11.30pm.

○ Make sure your camera flash is off. Safari personnel take this very seriously and have been known to stop rides because of flashers.

✕ **Take a Break**

Food and drink options abound outside the entrance. **Jungle Rotisserie** (Entrance Plaza; mains S$15-25; ⏲5.30-11pm; 🛜) serves fresh-from-the-oven roast chicken.

For local specialities, try **Ulu Ulu Safari Restaurant** (📞6360 8560; Entrance Plaza; buffet adult/child under 13 yr from S$29/19, mains S$17-36; ⏲5.30-10.30pm), with both à la carte options and a buffet.

★ **Getting There**

Catch the train to Ang Mo Kio MRT and then bus 138. It will cost about S$25 for a taxi from the CBD.

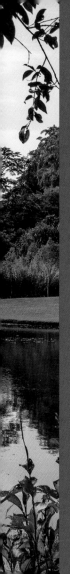

Explore

Holland Village, Dempsey Hill & the Botanic Gardens

Chic, salubrious Holland Village may not be a must for visitors, but its boutiques, cafes and 'lunching ladies' offer a revealing slice of expat life. Even leafier is historic Dempsey Hill, a converted barracks laced with antiques dealers, cafes and languid bistros. Upstaging them both is the Botanic Gardens, an invigorating blend of rare orchids and precious rainforest.

The Short List

○ **Singapore Botanic Gardens (p102)** *Taking deep, blissful breaths of air in Singapore's lush retreat.*

○ **National Orchid Garden (p103)** *Marvelling at the beauty, diversity and sheer quantity of varieties on display at this orchid showcase.*

○ **Dempsey Hill (p112)** *Shopping for unique home-wares in the area's antique shops and galleries.*

○ **Candlenut (p106)** *Savouring Michelin-starred Peranakan cuisine in colonial Dempsey Hill.*

Getting There & Around

Ⓜ Singapore Botanic Gardens and Holland Village both have their own MRT stations.

🚌 To reach Dempsey Hill catch bus 7, 75, 77, 105, 106, 123 or 174 from behind Orchard MRT, on Orchard Blvd. Get off two stops after the Singapore Botanic Gardens, then walk up to your left. Buses 75 and 106 are two of several linking Holland Village with Dempsey Hill.

Neighbourhood Map on p104

Singapore Botanic Gardens (p102) SIMONLONG/GETTY IMAGES ©

Top Sight 📷
Singapore Botanic Gardens

For instant stress relief, take a dose of the Singapore Botanic Gardens. At the tail end of Orchard Rd, Singapore's most famous sprawl of greenery offers more than just picnic-friendly lawns and lakes. It's home to ancient rainforest, themed gardens, rare orchids, free concerts and one of Singapore's most romantic nosh spots. Breathe in, breathe out.

◎ MAP P104, H5

☏ 1800 471 7300

www.nparks.gov.sg/sbg

1 Cluny Rd

admission free

⊙ 5am–midnight

🅿; 🚌 7, 75, 77, 105, 106, 123, 174; Ⓜ Botanic Gardens

National Orchid Garden

The Botanic Gardens' now famous orchid breeding began in 1928 and you can get the historical low-down at the **National Orchid Garden** (adult/child under 12yr S$5/free; ⏲8.30am-7pm, last entry 6pm). To date, its 3 hectares are home to over 1000 species and 2000 hybrids, and around 600 of them are on display – the largest showcase of tropical orchids on Earth.

Learning Forest

The newest addition to the gardens gives visitors even more forest habitat to explore. With its elevated walkways and plenty of boardwalks, you can practically walk on the swamp wetland's water or touch the leaves in the forest canopy. If you need a break, lay back in the canopy web, a spider-like web built into the elevated walkway, and relax to the sounds of the forest.

Ginger Garden

If you thought there was only one type of ginger, the compact **Ginger Garden** (admission free; ⏲5am-midnight) will set you straight. Located next to the National Orchid Garden, this 1-hectare space contains over 250 members of the Zingiberaceae family. It's also where you'll find ginger-centric restaurant Halia (p107). A supporting cast of plants include the little-known Lowiaceae, with their orchid-like flowers.

Jacob Ballas Children's Garden

A great place for kids to interact with the natural world around us. The interactive zones, including a sensory garden and 'Magic of Photosynthesis' (process in which plants make food), are super fun, There's lots of enjoyment to be had traversing the suspension and log bridges, discovering the forest adventure playground, and cooling off in the water-play feature.

★ Top Tips

○ Excellent, volunteer-run guided tours of the Botanic Gardens take place every Saturday. See the website for times and themes.

○ Check the website for free opera concerts, occasionally held at the Botanic Gardens' Symphony Lake.

○ Buy water when you see it, not when you need it: signage in the Botanic Gardens is not always consistent and backtracking is hardly fun, especially when you're thirsty.

✗ Take a Break

For a romantic meal among the Botanic Garden's ginger plants, grab a table at Halia (p107). Or for true alfresco dining order a picnic set from **Casa Verde** (Map p104, H3; ☎6467 7326; www.casaverde.com. sg; dishes S$8-20, pizza S$24; ⏲7.30am-7.30pm, to 8.30pm Sat & Sun; 👶🐾) and set up in a spot of your choosing.

A **B** **C** **D**

1

Holland Rd

11 ✕
8 ✕
18 🅐
15 🅐 Lorong Mambong
HOLLAND VILLAGE
Holland Ave
Jln Merah Saga
Lorong Liput
6 ✕
Ⓜ Holland Village

2

✕10
19 🅐
✕ 4
Holland Ave
Taman Warna

0   200 m
0   0.1 miles

King's R

3

Holland Rd

Farrer Rd

4

See Enlargement

HOLLAND VILLAGE
Jln Merah Saga
Ⓜ Holland Village
Taman Warna

Holland Rd

Jln Hitam Manis

5

Holland Ave

Queensway

Ridout Rd

For reviews see

👁	Top Sights	p102
✕	Eating	p106
🅖	Drinking	p110
🅐	Shopping	p111

Commonwealth Dr

6

Ⓝ 0   500 m
0   0.25 miles

A **B** **C** **D**

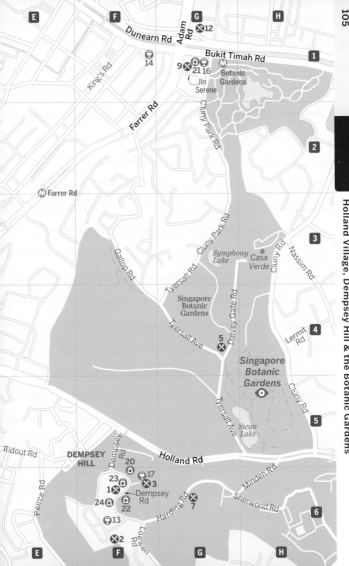

E
F
G
H

Dunearn Rd

Adam Rd

✕ 12

Bukit Timah Rd

1

14

9 ✕
21 16
M
Botanic Gardens

Jln Serene

King's Rd

Farrer Rd

Cluny Park Rd

2

M Farrer Rd

3

Cluny Park Rd

Symphony Lake

Casa Verde

Cluny Rd

Nassim Rd

Gallop Rd

Tyersall Rd

Singapore Botanic Gardens

Tyersall Ave

Dalvey Gate Rd

5 ✕

Lermit Rd

4

Singapore Botanic Gardens ◉

Cluny Rd

Tyersall Ave

Swan Lake

5

Ridout Rd

Holland Rd

DEMPSEY HILL

Dempsey Rd

20

Minden Rd

17

23
1 ✕
24
22

3

Dempsey Rd

Sherwood Rd

6

Peirce Rd

13

Harding Rd

7 ✕

✕ 2

Loewen Rd

E
F
G
H

Eating

Candlenut

PERANAKAN $$

1 ⊗ MAP P104, F6

The first and only Peranakan restaurant with a Michelin star, Candlenut is where Singaporeans head to impress out-of-towners. Chef Malcolm Lee does not churn out any old Straits Chinese dishes, instead he elevates them to new culinary heights. Most are amazing, but some are a little lost in translation. The jury is still out on whether Nonya would approve. (✆ 1800 304 2288; www.comodempsey.sg; Block 17A, Dempsey Rd; mains S$20-32; ⊙noon-2.30pm & 6-9.30pm, to 10.30pm Fri & Sat; 🚌7, 75, 77, 105, 106, 123, 174)

Chopsuey

CHINESE $$$

2 ⊗ MAP P104, F6

Swirling ceiling fans, crackly 1930s tunes and ladies on rattan chairs – Chopsuey has colonial chic down pat. It serves revamped versions of retro American-Chinese dishes, but the real highlight is the lunchtime yum cha; standouts include grilled pork and coconut salad, crispy lobster wontons, and *san choy pau* (minced meat in lettuce cups). The marble bar is perfect for solo diners. (✆ 6708 9288; www.chopsueycafe.com; 01-23, Block 10, Dempsey Rd; dumplings S$7-15, mains S$12-46; ⊙11.30am-10.30pm, from 10.30am Sat & Sun; 🚌7, 75, 77, 105, 106, 123, 174)

Long Beach Seafood

SEAFOOD $$

3 ⊗ MAP P104, F6

One of Singapore's top seafood restaurant chains. Settle in on the verandah, gaze out at the tropical greenery and tackle the cult-status black-pepper crab. The original Long Beach lays claim to inventing the iconic dish, and the version here is fantastically peppery and earthy. Best of all, the kitchen is open later than those of many restaurants in town. (✆ 6323 2222; www.longbeachseafood.com.sg; 01-01, Block 25, Dempsey Rd; mains S$12-22, crab per kg from S$78; ⊙11am-3pm & 5pm-1am; 🚌7, 75, 77, 105, 106, 123, 174)

Dempsey Cookhouse & Bar

BISTRO $$$

Visually stunning with a white-and-black colour scheme, a soaring ceiling dotted with oversized lantern lights, and touches of tropical greenery, there is a definite buzz in this restaurant (see 1 ⊗ Map p 104, F6) opened by one of New York's most celebrated chefs, Jean-Georges Vongerichten. Skip the signature egg caviar and opt for the creamy burrata (Italian semi-soft cheese) with lemon jam, followed by the spice-crusted snapper. (✆ 1800 304 5588; www.comodempsey.sg; Block 17D, Dempsey Rd; mains S$19-67; ⊙noon-2.30pm & 6-10pm, to 11pm Fri & Sat; 🚌7, 75, 77, 105, 106, 123, 174)

Halia

Blu Kouzina GREEK $$$

Opa! Stepping into this large, bustling restaurant (see 2  Map p104, F6) is like joining a large and very festive gathering. Plates of succulent meats, grilled seafood and flavourful salads are shared among guests at cosy and family-sized tables. Take a seat and get ordering – don't miss the *saganaki* (cheese) with figs, which you can wash down with decent Greek wine. (6875 0872; www.blukouzina.com; 01-21, Block 10, Dempsey Rd; dishes S$15-49, sharing platters from S$51; noon-2.30pm & 6-10pm; 7, 75, 77, 105, 106, 123, 174)

2am: dessertbar DESSERTS $$

4 MAP P104, B2

Posh desserts with wine and cocktail pairings is the deal at this swanky hideout. The menu includes savoury grub, like pork sliders and mac and cheese, but everyone comes here for Janice Wong's sweet show-stoppers, from chocolate tart to cassis plum bombe with elderflower yoghurt foam. Book ahead for Thursday to Saturday night. (6291 9727; www.2amdessertbar. com; 21A Lorong Liput; dishes S$15-24; 3pm-2am Tue-Fri, from 2pm Sat & Sun; Holland Village)

Halia FUSION $$$

5 MAP P104, G4

Atmospheric Halia is surrounded by the Botanic Gardens' ginger plants, a fact echoed in several unusual ginger-based dishes. Menus are a competent, fusion affair (think chilli-crab spaghettini), and the weekday set lunch (two/three courses S$28/34) is especially good value. There's a vegetarian and a kids' menu, and at weekends you can also do brunch (10am to 5pm); no reservations taken.

No alcohol is served, but it does refreshing fruit mocktails. (☎8444 1148; www.halia.com.sg; 1 Cluny Rd, Singapore Botanic Gardens; mains S$22-130; ⏱noon-9.30pm, from 5pm Sat & Sun; 🖬🚼; 🚌7, 75, 77, 105, 106, 123, 174, MBotanic Gardens)

Original Sin   VEGETARIAN $$

6 ✖ MAP P104, C1

Vibrant textiles, crisp linen and beautiful stemware set a smart, upbeat scene for sophisticated, flesh-free dishes like spicy, quinoa-stuffed roasted capsicum, and Middle Eastern eggplant moussaka. The restaurant is on a residential street dotted with eating options; book an outdoor table if possible. (☎6475 5605; www.originalsin.com.sg; 01-62, 43 Jln Merah Saga; mains S$24-29; ⏱11.30am-2.30pm & 6-10pm; 🖬; MHolland Village)

White Rabbit   INTERNATIONAL $$$

7 ✖ MAP P104, G6

Dempsey Hill's 1930s Ebenezer chapel has been reborn as a sophisticated, whitewashed dining room and bar. Find the light in tweaked Euro comforters like tagliatelle with Alaskan king crab and 36-hour short ribs with ruby port glaze. Weekend brunch (10.30am to 3pm) includes breakfast staples like eggs and waffles but mixes things up with oysters and wagyu burgers.

Hop on outside to the Rabbit Hole garden bar to enjoy a refreshing craft gin and homemade tonic. (☎6473 9965; www.thewhiterabbit.com.sg; 39C Harding Rd; 2-/3-course set lunch S$38/42, mains S$28-65;

Tanglin Barracks

The area now known as Dempsey Hill was the site of Tanglin Barracks, one of the first barracks constructed in Singapore. Opened in 1861 the original buildings were spacious, elevated wooden structures topped with thatched *attap* (sugar-palm) roofs and able to house 50 men. Among the barracks' amenities were hospital wards, wash houses, kitchens, a library, a reading room and a school, as well as office quarters. Extensive renovation between 1934 and 1936 saw the airy verandahs make way for more interior space, though the French-tiled roofs – which had replaced the original thatched ones – were, thankfully, preserved. Home to the British military for over a century, the barracks served as the headquarters of the Ministry of Defence between 1972 and 1989, before their current reinvention as an upmarket lunch hang-out.

noon-2.30pm & 6.30-10.30pm Tue-Fri, from 10.30am Sat & Sun; 🚌 7, 75, 77, 105, 106, 123, 174)

Sunday Folks
DESSERTS $$

8 ✖️ MAP P104, C1

A sugar rush is a given at this airy, industrial-style dessert cafe where every delectable treat is hand-made. Folks flock here for the fluffy waffles crowned with a towering swirl of decadent soft-serve ice cream. Choose one of four ice-cream flavours – our pick is the sweet-and-savoury sea-salt *gula melaka* (palm sugar) – and then go nuts with toppings. (📞 6479 9166; www.sundayfolks.com; 01-52, 44 Jln Merah Saga; waffles S$10-20; 🕐 1-10pm Tue-Thu, from noon Fri-Sun; Ⓜ Holland Village)

The Bakery by Woodlands Sourdough
BAKERY $

9 ✖️ MAP P104, G1

Everything on this bakery's short menu comes with the disclaimer 'till sell out', so you've been warned! Husband and wife Nur and Chalith set up shop after demand for their sourdough bread delivery service went ballistic; now loyal customers have to come to them and they do, in droves! Join the queue and order what you can – it's all amazing. (www.woodlandssourdough.bigcartel.com; 01-05 Serene Centre, 10 Jln Serene; sandwiches S$9; 🕐 8.30am-6pm Wed-Sun; 🖋️; Ⓜ Botanic Gardens)

Island Creamery
ICE CREAM $

10 ✖️ MAP P104, B2

A calorific shrine for many Singaporeans, who don't mind queuing at this tiny shop for its freshly made ice creams, sorbets and pies. Keep it local with flavours including *teh tarik* (sweet spiced Indian tea) and the wonderful Tiger beer sorbet, or get nostalgic over the Milo or Horlicks concoctions. (📞 6468 8859; www.islandcreamery.com; 19 Lorong Liput; 🕐 noon-10pm, to 11pm Fri & Sat; Ⓜ Holland Village)

Da Paolo Pizza Bar
ITALIAN $$

11 ✖️ MAP P104, C1

The successful Da Paolo chain has two outlets in Holland Village alone: a deli-cafe (at 118 Holland Ave) and this polished bistro with terrace seating. Under a cowhide ceiling, svelte expats dine on delicious thin-crust pizzas, competent pastas and warm chocolate brownies. There's a good-value weekday set lunch (S$23) and one-for-one happy hour noon to 2.30pm and 5.30pm to 7.30pm. (📞 6479 6059; www.dapaolo.com.sg; 01-46, 44 Jln Merah Saga; pizzas S$20-31, pasta S$22-28; 🕐 noon-2.30pm & 5.30-10.30pm Mon-Fri, 11am-10.30pm Sat & Sun; Ⓜ Holland Village)

Adam Road Food Centre
HAWKER $

12 ✖️ MAP P104, G1

Locals tout this hawker centre as home to the best *nasi lemak* (coconut rice served with fried anchovies, peanuts and a curry dish) in town.

Join the line at Selera Rasa Nasi Lemak (stall 01-02) to taste the dish rumoured to have been served to Indonesian president Joko Widodo by Singapore's prime minister, Lee Hsien Loong, in 2014. (cnr Adam & Dunearn Rds; dishes from S$2.50; ⏰7am-2am; Ⓜ Botanic Gardens)

Drinking

Green Door   BAR

13 Ⓜ MAP P104, F6

Wide sky, sinuous palms and the odd frangipani breeze: slip behind the green door for a little tropical seduction. Under gramophone lights, barkeepers shake and stir cocktails splashed with herbs and fruit straight from the garden, of which the Garden Goddess is particularly refreshing. Early-bird specials (5pm to 8pm daily) are decent, pulling in a languid expat crowd. (📞6776 0777; www.theprive group.com.sg; Block 13A, Dempsey Rd; ⏰5pm-midnight, to 1am Fri & Sat, 1pm-midnight Sun; 📶; 🚌7, 75, 77, 105, 106, 123, 174)

Atlas Coffeehouse   COFFEE

14 Ⓜ MAP P104, F1

This airy industrial-styled coffee-house has caffeine lovers lining up for the in-house Guatemalan and Brazilian bean blend by Two Degrees North Coffee Co. Like your coffee served cold? Try the Black Bird, a taste flight of cold brew, nitro brew and iced black – perfect on a hot day. (📞6314 2674; www.atlascoffeehouse.com.sg;

6 Duke's Rd; ⏰8am-6.30pm Tue-Sun; Ⓜ Botanic Gardens)

Wala Wala Café Bar   BAR

15 Ⓜ MAP P104, A1

Perennially packed at weekends (and most evenings, too), Wala Wala has live music on the 2nd floor, with warm-up acts Monday to Friday from 7pm and main acts nightly from 9.30pm. Downstairs it pulls in football fans with its large sports screens. As at most nearby places, tables spill out onto the street in the evenings. (📞6462 4288; www.wala wala.sg; 31 Lorong Mambong; ⏰4pm-1am Mon-Thu, to 2am Fri, 3pm-2am Sat, 3pm-1am Sun; Ⓜ Holland Village)

Gastronomia   CAFE

16 Ⓜ MAP P104, G1

Directly across the road from the Botanic Gardens MRT station, this casual coffeeshop is a perfect pit stop before or after your garden visit. Pull up a chair on the breezy verandah or grab a coffee to go and head upstairs to explore the trendy fashion and homewares boutiques geared towards the local expat community. (📞6468 7010; www.dapaolo.com.sg; 01-01 Cluny Ct, 501 Bukit Timah Rd; ⏰7.30am-10pm; Ⓜ Botanic Gardens)

RedDot Brewhouse   MICROBREWERY

17 Ⓜ MAP P104, F6

In a quiet spot in Dempsey Hill, RedDot has been pouring its own microbrews for years. Ditch

A Virtuous Morning

If you feel like stretching your limbs, join the early morning fitness fanatics who descend on the Botanic Gardens (p102) from sunrise to stroll, run, roll out yoga mats and submit to bootcamp instructors. Keep an eye out for the mesmerising tai chi classes; the ones using fans or swords are the best. You'll find plenty of shelters in case the heavens open, but water fountains are hard to locate, so bring your own water bottle. Workout done, reward yourself with breakfast at Casa Verde (p103) at the Nassim Gate Visitors Centre, or Gastronomia (p110) just outside the Bukit Timah gate, the latter conveniently situated next to the Botanic Gardens MRT.

the average food and focus on the suds, sipped to the sound of screeching parrots. There are eight beers on tap (S$12 for a pint), including an eye-catching, spirulina-spiked green lager. Happy hour runs from noon to 7pm, with S$9 pints. (☑6475 0500; www.reddotbrewhouse.sg; 01-01, Block 25A, Dempsey Rd; ☺noon-midnight, to 2am Fri & Sat, 10am-midnight Sun; 🚌7, 75, 77, 105, 106, 123, 174)

Shopping

Bynd Artisan ARTS & CRAFTS

18 🅐 MAP P104, C1

Connoisseurs of bespoke stationery and leather will love this sublime store that prides itself on artisanal excellence. Select from the range of handmade journals or spend time customising your own; don't forget to deboss your name. Other items include leather travel accessories and jewellery pieces. For the complete artist

experience, sign up for a course (from S$78) in leather crafting or bookbinding. (☑6475 1680; www.byndartisan.com; 01-54, 44 Jln Merah Saga; ☺noon-9pm, from 10am Sat & Sun; Ⓜ Holland Village)

Holland Road Shopping Centre MALL

19 🅐 MAP P104, B2

Holland Road Shopping Centre remains a magnet for expats seeking art, handicrafts, homewares and offbeat fashion. Dive into **Lim's** (☑6466 3188; www.facebook.com/limshollandvillage; ☺10am-8pm) for some good Asian–inspired finds or scour the shelves of **Independent Market** (☑6466 5534; www.independentmarket.sg; ☺noon-7pm Mon-Sat, 1-6pm Sun) for a quirky Singapore-an souvenir. Shopped out? Hit the nail spas or massage parlours, which are dotted over the two levels. (211 Holland Ave; ☺10am-8.30pm; Ⓜ Holland Village)

Shang Antique ANTIQUES

20 🔒 MAP P104, F6

Specialising in antique religious artefacts from Cambodia, Laos, Thailand, India and Myanmar (Burma), as well as reproductions, Shang Antique has items dating back nearly 2000 years – with price tags to match. Those with more style than savings can pick up old bronze gongs, beautiful Thai silk scarves or Burmese ornamental rice baskets for under S$50. (📞 6388 8838; www.shangantique.com.sg; 01-03, Block 26, Dempsey Rd; 🕙 10am-7pm; 🚌 7, 75, 77, 105, 106, 123, 174)

Bungalow 55 HOMEWARES

21 🔒 MAP P104, G1

Colonial chic hits overdrive in this beautifully curated store brimming with chinoiserie lamps, tropical-scented candles, overstuffed cushions and everything a Singapore–based host-with-the-most would need in their life. Wander around and imagine relaxing on the verandah sipping G&Ts from your well-stocked cane bar cart – don't forget a Panama hat for the complete experience. (📞 6463 3831; www.thebungalow55.com; 01-05A, Cluny Court, 501 Bukit Timah Rd; 🕙 10am-7pm, to 5pm Sun; Ⓜ Botanic Gardens)

Expat Heavy Holland Village

Nonpermanent residents make up just under 30% of Singapore's population of 5.6 million residents, up from around 25% in 2000.

While many are low-paid construction and service-industry workers from China and South and Southeast Asia, a huge number are highly skilled professionals working in areas as diverse as finance, oil and gas, IT, biomedical science and academia, as well as tourism and hospitality. Indeed, one in four skilled workers in Singapore is foreign.

There are over 40,000 British nationals in Singapore alone, with other large communities including Australians, Americans, French and Japanese. Popular expat neighbourhoods include Orchard, Tanglin, Novena, Holland Village, Bukit Timah and the East Coast.

It's a thriving, vibrant scene, with no shortage of social and sporting clubs, international schools and expat magazines and websites. For many, Singapore's appeal is obvious: low crime, lower taxes, world-class healthcare and education, affordable domestic help and superlative international connections. Increasingly less appealing, however, is the soaring cost of living, made worse by the increasing number of companies moving away from all-inclusive expat packages to less-lucrative local contracts.

Em Gallery
FASHION, HOMEWARES

22 🔒 MAP P104, F6

Singapore-based Japanese designer Emiko Nakamura keeps Dempsey's society women looking whimsically chic in her light, sculptural creations. Emiko also collaborates with hill tribes in Laos to create naturally dyed hand-woven handicrafts, such as bags and cushions. Other homewares might include limited-edition (and reasonably priced) pottery from Cambodia. (☎6475 6941; www.emtradedesign.com; 01-03A Block 26, Dempsey Rd; ⏱10am-7pm, from 11am Sat & Sun; 🚌7, 75, 77, 105, 106, 123, 174)

Dover Street Market
FASHION & ACCESSORIES

23 🔒 MAP P104, F6

Singapore's fashion elite, with the very deepest of pockets, peruse the racks of this outpost of famous London fashion retailer. The ginormous warehouse space has been sectioned off with metal cage-like dividers, which make it feel like you're getting lost in a maze of high fashion. Labels include Gucci, Balenciaga, Comme des Garçons, Sara Lanzi and Sacai. (☎6304 1388; https://singapore.doverstreetmarket.com; Block 18, Dempsey Rd; ⏱11am-8pm; 🚌7, 75, 77, 105, 106, 123, 174)

Pasardina Fine Living
ANTIQUES, HOMEWARES

24 🔒 MAP P104, F6

If you plan on giving your home a tropical Asian makeover, this rambling treasure trove is a good starting point. Inspired by traditional Indonesian design, its collection includes beautiful teak furniture, ceramic and wooden statues, bark lampshades and the odd wooden archway. (☎6472 0228; www.facebook.com/pasardinafineliving; 01-01, Block 13, Demspey Rd; ⏱noon-6.30pm, to 7.30pm Sat & Sun; 🚌7, 75, 77, 105, 106, 123, 174)

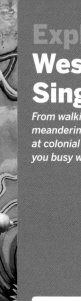

Explore

West & Southwest Singapore

From walking the stunning Southern Ridges to meandering through fabulous, and free, art galleries at colonial Gillman Barracks, there's plenty to keep you busy west of the CBD.

The Short List

○ **Southern Ridges (p116)** *Stretching your legs for a park-to-park walk along the lush Southern Ridges to Mt Faber, then hopping onto the cable car for sensational views.*

○ **Gillman Barracks (p120)** *Immersing yourself in culture, art and food while wandering around colonial gem Gillman Barracks.*

○ **Haw Par Villa (p121)** *Reliving a little 1950s tourism at this wonderfully quirky, more than slightly scary, theme park.*

Getting There & Around

Ⓜ HarbourFront, Jurong East, Boon Lay, Chinese Garden, Pioneer and Kranji are all useful stations within walking distance of sights or with bus connections to them.

Neighbourhood Map on p118

Haw Par Villa (p121) SIRAPHAT/SHUTTERSTOCK ©

Top Sight 📷
Southern Ridges

A series of parks and hills connecting Mt Faber to West Coast Park, the Southern Ridges brings the jungle to the heart of the city. The best stretch of the 10km route is from Kent Ridge Park to Mt Faber. It's relatively easy, and serves up some stunning sights, from skyline and jungle vistas to a seriously striking, wave-like walkway.

◎ MAP P118, D4

☎ 1800 471 7300

www.nparks.gov.sg

🕓 24hr

🅿

Ⓜ Pasir Panjang

Reflections at Bukit Chandu

Commemorating the last stand of the Malay Regiment against the Japanese in 1942, **Reflections at Bukit Chandu** (☑ 6375 2510; www.nhb. gov.sg; 31K Pepys Rd; admission free; ☺9am-5.30pm Tue-Sun) combines firsthand accounts, personal artefacts and films to describe the fierce battle that almost wiped out the regiment.

Kent Ridge Park

Behind Reflections at Bukit Chandu you'll find **Kent Ridge Park** (Vigilante Dr; ☺24hr). It's strangely deserted so you'll have its short, yet wonderful, canopy walk pretty much to yourself. From here, stroll downhill to **HortPark** (33 Hyderabad Rd; ☺6am-10pm; 🚻).

Forest Walk

A leaf-like bridge crosses over Alexandra Rd from HortPark, leading to the superb Forest Walk. While you can opt for the Earth trail, the Elevated Walkway is more appealing, offering eye-level views of the jungle canopy covering **Telok Blangah Hill** (Telok Blangah Green; ☺24hr).

Henderson Waves

The remarkable Henderson Waves, a rippling walkway soaring high above the forest floor, sits between Telok Blangah Hill Park and Mt Faber Park. The towers that seem to rise straight out of the jungle are part of Reflections at Keppel Bay – a residential development designed by world-renowned architect Daniel Libeskind.

Mt Faber

Rising 105m above the southern fringe of the city, Mt Faber's terraced trails wind past strategically positioned viewpoints. It's here you'll find the **cable-car service** (☑ 6377 9688; www.onefabergroup.com; adult/child return S$33/22; ☺8.45am-9.30pm) to HarbourFront and Sentosa.

★ Top Tips

○ The best time to hit the trail is late afternoon. This way you can avoid the worst of the midday heat and make it to Mt Faber in time for sunset drinks or dinner.

○ Wear comfortable shoes, sunglasses and a hat. Always bring plenty of water, and don't forget to pack an umbrella.

○ Bring your camera. The walk delivers beautiful views of the city, jungle and South China Sea.

○ If you encounter monkeys, do not feed them. This only encourages them to pester humans.

✕ Take a Break

For drinks and bistro fare with breathtaking city views, head to **Dusk** (p124). For more casual bites, opt for **Spuds & Aprons** (☑ 6377 9688; www. onefabergroup. com; 109 Mt Faber Rd; mains S$14-40; ☺11am-10pm; 🚋Mt Faber). Both are atop Mt Faber.

A **B** 9 **C** **D**

Commonwealth M

1 3 2 Lee Kong Chian
Natural History Museum
NUS
Museum

Dover Rd

Portsdown Rd

Ayer Rajah Expwy (AYE)

6 Ayer Rajah Cr

Whitchurch
Rd

2 National
University
of Singapore

Kent Ridge M

11

13 Science Park Dr

Ayer Rajah Expwy (AYE)

Portsdown Ave

Pasir Panjang Rd

West Coast Hwy

3 Buona Vista South Rd

Kent
Ridge
Park

4 Haw Par
Villa

Southern
Ridges

Haw Par
M Villa

Jln Mat Jambol

4 Pasir
Panjang
Terminal

Pasir Panjang Rd

Pepys Rd

Pasir M
Panjang

West Coast Hwy

PASIR
PANJANG

5

For reviews see

	Top Sights	p116
	Sights	p120
	Eating	p122
	Drinking	p123
	Shopping	p124

N 0 ————————— 1 km
0 ————————— 0.5 mile

Sebarok Channel

6

A **B** **C** **D**

E
F
G
H

Queensway

DEMPSEY HILL

Loewen Rd

Grange Rd

1

Chatsworth Rd

Commonwealth Ave

QUEENSTOWN

Bishopgate

Tanglin Rd

Jervois Rd

2

Queensway

Singapore River

Tiong Bahru Rd

Alexandra Rd

Redhill Ⓜ

Delta Stadium

Alexandra Rd

Jln Tiong

Tiong Bahru Rd

Henderson Rd

3

Lower Delta Rd

Jln Bukit Merah

Ayer Rajah Expwy (AYE)

Depot Rd

4

12 🏛

1 ◉ Gillman Barracks

Telok Blangah Hill Park

Alexandra Rd

Lock Rd

Henderson Rd

Mt Faber Cable Car Station

16 🔒

✕ 8

Lower Delta Rd

Telok Blangah Dr

5

Ⓜ Labrador Park

Mt Faber Park ▲ Mt Faber

Labrador Villa Rd

Telok Blangah Ⓜ

West Coast Hwy

14 ◉

7 ✕

Port Rd

10 ✕

HarbourFront Cable Car Station 🚠

HarbourFront

Ⓜ

5 ◉ Labrador Nature Reserve

Keppel Harbour

15 ◉ Pulau Keppel

17 🔒

VivoCity

6

Sentosa Gateway

E
F
G
H

Sights

Gillman Barracks GALLERY

1 ◎ MAP P118, E4

A former British military encampment, Gillman Barracks now houses a contemporary arts hub set in a lush landscape. Among its 11 galleries is New York's **Sundaram Tagore** (☏6694 3378; www.sundaramtagore. com; 01-05, 5 Lock Rd; admission free; ⏱11am-7pm Tue-Sat), which represents big names such as Annie Leibovitz. Also on-site is the **NTU Centre for Contemporary Art** (☏6339 6503; www.ntu.ccasingapore. org; Block 43, Malan Rd; admission free; ⏱noon-7pm Tue-Thu, Sat & Sun, to 9pm Fri), a forward-thinking art-research centre hosting art talks, lectures and contemporary exhibitions from dynamic regional and international artists working in a variety of media. Individual gallery hours vary.

To reach Gillman Barracks, catch the MRT to Labrador Park station and walk north up Alexandra Rd for 800m; the entry to Gillman Barracks is on your right. A one-way taxi fare from the CBD will set you back around S$12. (www.gillmanbarracks.com; 9 Lock Rd; admission free; ⏱11am-7pm Tue-Sun; P; MLabrador Park)

Lee Kong Chian Natural History Museum MUSEUM

2 ◎ MAP P118, A1

What looks like a giant rock bursting with greenery is actually Singapore's high-tech, child-friendly natural history museum. The main Biodiversity Gallery delves into the origin of life using a stimulating combo of fossils, taxidermy and interactive displays. Hard to miss are Prince, Apollonia and Twinky: three 150-million-year-old Diplodocid sauropod dinosaur skeletons, two with their original skulls. Upstairs, the Heritage Gallery explores the collection's 19th-century origins, with an interesting section on Singapore's geology to boot. (☏6601 3333; http://lkcnhm.nus. edu.sg; 2 Conservatory Dr; adult/child under 13yr S$21/13; ⏱10am-7pm Tue-Sun; P; ☐96)

NUS Museum MUSEUM

3 ◎ MAP P118, A1

Located on the verdant campus of the National University of Singapre (NUS), this museum is one of the city's lesser-known cultural delights. Ancient Chinese ceramics and bronzes, as well as archaeological fragments found in Singapore, dominate the ground-floor Lee Kong Chian Collection; one floor up, the South and Southeast Asian Gallery showcases paintings, sculpture and textiles from the region. The Ng Eng Teng Collection is dedicated to Ng Eng Teng (1934–2001), Singapore's foremost modern artist, best known for his figurative sculptures. (☏6516 8817; www.museum.nus.edu. sg; National University of Singapore, 50 Kent Ridge Cres; admission free; ⏱10am-6pm Tue-Sat; P; ☐96)

Haw Par Villa

MUSEUM, PARK

4 ◉ MAP P118, B3

The refreshingly weird and kitsch Haw Par Villa was the brainchild of Aw Boon Haw, the creator of the medicinal salve Tiger balm. After Aw Boon Haw built a villa here in 1937 for his beloved brother and business partner, Aw Boon Par, the siblings began building a Chinese-mythology theme park within the grounds. Top billing goes to the Ten Courts of Hell (closes at 5.45pm), a walk-through exhibit depicting the gruesome torments awaiting sinners in the underworld. (☏6773 0103; www.hawparvilla. sg; 262 Pasir Panjang Rd; admission free; ☉9am-7pm, last entry 6pm; P; MHaw Par Villa)

Labrador Nature Reserve

PARK

5 ◉ MAP P118, E6

Combining forest trails rich in birdlife and a beachfront park, Labrador Park is also scattered with evocative British war relics, only rediscovered in the 1980s. Look out for old gun emplacements mounted on moss-covered concrete casements, as well as for the remains of the entrance to the old fort that once stood guard on this hill. The reserve's hilly terrain sweeps down to the shore, where expansive lawns, shade and the sound of lapping waves invite a lazy picnic. (☏1800 471 7300; www.nparks.gov.sg; Labrador Villa Rd; ☉24hr; P; MLabrador Park)

NUS Museum

MERVIN CHUA/LONELY PLANET ©

Eating

Timbre+

HAWKER $

6  MAP P118, C2

Welcome to the new generation of hawker centres. With over 30 food outlets, Timbre+ has it all: artwork-covered shipping containers, Airstream trailer food trucks, craft beer and live music nightly. But it's the food that draws the crowds: a mixture of traditional and New Age. Head here in the late afternoon before the old-school hawker stalls shut at 6pm. (📞6252 2545; www.timbre plus.sg; JTC LaunchPad@one-north, 73A Ayer Rajah Cres; dishes from S$3; ⏲6am-midnight Mon-Thu, to 1am Fri & Sat, 11am-10pm Sun, stall hours vary; Ⓜ One North)

Tamarind Hill

THAI $$$

7  MAP P118, E6

In a colonial bungalow in Labrador Park, Tamarind Hill sets an elegant scene for exceptional Thai. The highlight is the Sunday brunch (S$60; noon to 3pm), a buffet of beautiful cold dishes and salads plus as many dishes from the à la carte menu as you like. Book ahead. (📞6278 6364; www. tamarindrestaurants.com; 30 Labrador Villa Rd; mains S$18-59; ⏲noon-2.30pm Mon-Sat, 11.30am-3pm Sun, 6.30-9.45pm Sun-Thu, to 10.30pm Fri & Sat; 🛜; Ⓜ Labrador Park)

Naked Finn

SEAFOOD $$$

8  MAP P118, E5

You'll find this slinky pocket rocket at the commercial gallery hub,

Timbre+

RIA DE JONG/LONELY PLANET ©

Gillman Barracks. It's located in a glass-like box, with lush greenery wall, and serves up super-fresh seafood dishes in pared-down style. If you're there for lunch be sure to order the lobster roll, raved about all over Singapore – sadly it's not available at dinner. (☑6694 0807; www.nakedfinn.com; 39 Malan Rd, Gillman Barracks; mains S$30-78; ☺noon-2.30pm Tue-Sat, 6-9pm Tue-Thu, to 9.30pm Fri & Sat; Ⓜ Labrador Park)

Masons INTERNATIONAL $$

Located on the grounds of Gillman Barracks (see 1 ◎ Map p118, E4), this cafe-bistro comes with high ceilings, elegant verandah seating and a marble bar with black leather sofas for a post-gallery cocktail (happy hour 4pm to 7pm). Italian flavours dominate the menu, accompanied by American staples including bourbon-smoked ribs and juicy beef burgers. Herbivores will appreciate the dedicated vegetarian options. (☑6694 2216; www.masons.sg; 8 Lock Rd, Gillman Barracks; mains S$18-38; ☺noon-11pm; 🖋; Ⓜ Labrador Park)

Wuerstelstand HAWKER $

9 ⓧ MAP P118, B1

Erich, an eccentric Austrian chef, hawks low-priced sausages and sauerkraut from what he proclaims to be 'the last sausage kiosk before the equator'. Just follow the smell of fresh baked pretzels and grilling sausages.

Loved by European expats and locals alike. (☑9627 4081; www.backstube.sg; 01-97, 7 Stars Coffee Shop, Block 28, Dover Cres; sausages from S$3; ☺9am-2pm & 5.30-9pm; Ⓜ Dover)

PeraMakan PERANAKAN $$

10 ⓧ MAP P118, F6

Run by a genial couple of cooking enthusiasts, this paragon of homestyle Baba-Nonya cuisine migrated from its spiritual Joo Chiat home. Thankfully, classics such as sambal squid and *rendang* remain as plate-lickingly good as ever. One dish you don't want to miss is the ayam buah keluak (chicken in a rich spicy sauce served with Indonesian black-nut pulp). (☑6377 2829; www.peramakan.com; Level 3, Keppel Club, 10 Bukit Chermin Rd; mains S$14-25; ☺11.30am-2pm & 6-9pm; 🅿🖋; Ⓜ Telok Blangah)

Drinking

Colbar BAR

11 🍺 MAP P118, D2

Raffish Colbar is an evocative colonial throwback, a former British officers' mess turned languid drinking spot. It's still 1950-something here, a place where money is kept in a drawer, football team photos hang on the wall and locals linger over beers and well-priced ciders on the spacious verandah. (☑6779 4859; 9A Whitchurch Rd; ☺11am-10pm Tue-Sun; 🚌191)

Handlebar   PUB

12 🚇 MAP P118, E4

You might not expect to find a biker bar sitting alongside fancy art galleries and top-notch restaurants, but here Handlebar is. There are usually more families here than motorheads, and it makes a lovely place for a few drinks in the cool of the afternoon. The daiquiris made in blenders fashioned out of petrol engines go down a treat. (☏6268 5550; www.handlebaroriginal.com; Block 10, Lock Rd, Gillman Barracks; ⏰noon-midnight Tue-Thu & Sun, to 1am Fri & 2am Sat; Ⓜ Labrador Park)

Good Beer Company   CRAFT BEER

13 🚇 MAP P118, B2

After injecting Chinatown Complex (p148) with a dose of new-school cool, this hawker-centre beer stall made the move in September 2017 to much bigger digs, just minutes from the National University of Singapore. With eight craft beers on tap and an impressive booty of bottled craft suds, sourced from far-flung corners of the world, it's a brew enthusiast's paradise. (☏9430 2750; www.facebook.com/goodbeersg; 01-23 Savourworld, 2 Science Park Dr; ⏰4-11pm Mon-Thu, to 11.45pm Fri & Sat; Ⓜ Kent Ridge)

Dusk   BAR

14 🚇 MAP P118, H5

Perched atop Mt Faber, Dusk has a sweeping view over Harbour-Front to Sentosa Island and the Strait of Singapore beyond. Sunset is the perfect time to enjoy the sky's changing hues as you sit, cocktail in hand. (☏6377 9688; www.onefabergroup.com; 109 Mt Faber Rd; ⏰4-11pm Mon-Thu, to 2am Fri & Sat, 11am-11pm Sun; 🚠Mt Faber)

Privé Keppel Bay   BAR

15 🚇 MAP P118, F6

You couldn't ask for a better setting for morning coffee or evening drinks: this bar is located on an island out in the middle of Keppel Harbour, with the city on one side and Sentosa Island on the other. Happy hour runs from 5pm to 8pm daily. Attracts an affluent, well-dressed crowd looking to unwind by the water. (☏6776 0777; www. theprivegroup.com.sg; Marina at Keppel Bay, 2 Keppel Bay Vista; ⏰9am-midnight Mon-Fri, from 8am Sat & Sun; Ⓜ HarbourFront)

Shopping

Dustbunny Vintage   VINTAGE

16 🏠 MAP P118, H5

This vintage veteran is not in the most convenient location, tucked away on a HDB (Housing and Development Board) estate, but the well-curated collection of dresses, handbags and accessories has made it a must-shop if you're on the lookout for great-value designer finds. Boutique owner Pia revels in helping shoppers find the perfect pieces to add to their collections. (☏6274 4200; 01-203,

VivoCity

Block 112, Bukit Purmei Rd; ⊙12.30-8.30pm Mon-Fri, 1-7pm Sat, 1-5pm Sun by appointment; 🚌123, 131)

VivoCity   MALL

17 🔒 MAP P118, H6

More than just Singapore's largest shopping mall, VivoCity offers that rare commodity: open space.

There's an outdoor kids' playground on level two and a rooftop 'skypark' where little ones can splash about in free-to-use paddling pools. The retail mix is predominantly mid-range, and there's a large Golden Village cineplex. (📞6377 6860; www.vivocity.com.sg; 1 HarbourFront Walk; ⊙10am-10pm; 📶👶; Ⓜ HarbourFront, 🚝Sentosa Express)

Explore
Sentosa Island

Epitomised by its star attraction, Universal Studios, Sentosa is essentially one giant Pleasure Island. The choices are head-spinning, from duelling roller coasters and indoor skydiving to fake surf and luge racing. Add to this a historic fort, state-of-the-art aquarium and Ibiza-inspired beachside bars and restaurants and it's clear why locals head here to live a little

The Short List

∘ **Universal Studios (p128)** *Indulging your inner child at Singapore's blockbuster theme park, home to warrior mummies, bad-tempered dinosaurs and the world's tallest duelling roller coasters.*

∘ **SEA Aquarium (p131)** *Visiting the adorable, the curious and the deadly at the world's largest aquarium.*

∘ **Tanjong Beach Club (p134)** *Feeling the sand between your toes and the breeze on your face as you toast the sunset with the party set.*

∘ **Knolls (p134)** *Popping the champagne and eating till your heart's content at the free-flow Sunday brunch.*

Getting There & Around

🚡 Ride to/from Mt Faber or the HarbourFront Centre to Sentosa Station on the island. On Sentosa, a separate cable-car line, the Sentosa Line, stops at Imbiah Lookout, Merlion and Siloso Point.

🚝 The Sentosa Express monorail goes from VivoCity to three stations on Sentosa: Waterfront, Imbiah and Beach.

🚶 Simply walk across the Sentosa Boardwalk from VivoCity.

🚌 Sentosa is serviced by free 'beach tram' (an electric bus) shuttles, and buses.

Neighbourhood Map on p130

Top Sight 📷
Universal Studios

The top draw in sprawling Resorts World (an integrated resort on Sentosa Island) is Universal Studios. It offers a booty of rides, roller coasters, shows, shops and restaurants, all neatly packaged into fantasy-world themes based on your favourite Hollywood films. Attractions span both the toddler-friendly and the seriously gut-wrenching.

◎ MAP P130, E2

📞 6577 8888

www.rwsentosa.com

Resorts World, 8 Sentosa Gateway

adult/child under 13yr S$76/56

🕙 10am-7pm

🚊 Waterfront

Battlestar Galactica

If you're a hard-core thrill seeker, strap yourself into Battlestar Galactica, which consists of the world's tallest duelling roller coasters. Choose between the sit-down HUMAN roller coaster and the CYLON, an inverted roller coaster with multiple loops and flips. If you can pull your attention away from the screaming (yours and others'), be sure to enjoy the bird's-eye view.

Revenge of the Mummy

The main attraction of the park's Ancient Egypt section, Revenge of the Mummy will have you twisting, dipping and hopping in darkness in your search for the Book of the Living. Contrary to Hollywood convention, your journey will end with a surprising, fiery twist.

Transformers: The Ride

This exhilarating, next-generation motion thrill ride deploys high-definition 3D animation to transport you to a dark, urban other-world where you'll be battling giant robots, engaging in high-speed chases, and even plunging off the edge of a soaring skyscraper. It's an incredibly realistic, adrenaline-pumping experience.

Puss in Boots' Giant Journey

Perfect for little kids, this suspended roller coaster takes you on a fairly tame ride with Puss in Boots and his girlfriend, Kitty Softpaws, in search of Mother Goose's precious golden egg. The attention to detail is wonderful; sit in the last row for more of a thrill.

WaterWorld

Gripping stunts and fiery explosions are what you get at WaterWorld, a spectacular live show based on the Kevin Costner flick. Head here at least 20 minutes before show time if you want a decent seat. Those wanting a drenching should sit in the soak zone, right at the front.

★ Top Tips

○ If lining up isn't your thing, it may be worth investing in an express pass (from S$30), which lets you jump in the fast lane once for each participating ride.

○ Lockers are available around the park, so you don't have to lug everything around with you all day. A small locker (S$15) is the perfect size for a backpack.

✗ Take a Break

For those travelling with a tribe, head to **Loui's NY Pizza Parlor** (New York Zone; large pizza S$50; ⊕10am-7pm) for a humongous, tasty pizza.

Want to leave Universal Studios? Head just outside the main entrance to Malaysian Food Street (p133). Make sure to get a stamp on your hand if you want to re-enter the theme park.

Sentosa Island

Pulau
Brani

Selat Sengkir

Brani Terminal Ave

Sentosa Gateway

Causeway Bridge

Keppel Harbour

Siloso Rd

Fort Siloso **1**

Siloso Point

Siloso Point **X 12**

Siloso Beach

AJ Hackett Bungy **X**
Wave House **9**

Mt Imbiah
Imbiah Walk

Imbiah Lookout

Sentosa Cable Car Station

Adventure Cove Waterpark **6**

SEA Aquarium

Merlion Plaza

Waterfront **Resorts World**

Gateway Ave

Universal Studios

The Knolls

Serapong Golf Course

Allanbrooke Rd

Bukit Manis Rd

Tanjong Golf Course

Tanjong Beach

Tanjong Beach **13**

X 10
14

Palawan Beach

Beach View

Artillery Ave

KidZania **5**

Merlion **7**

Imbiah **8**

Images of Singapore Live **3**

Siloso Beach **15**
Skyline Luge Sentosa **16**

Beach **8**

Sebarok Channel

X 11 3

Palawan Beach

The Knolls

For reviews see
◎ Top Sights   p128
◉ Sights   p131
✕ Eating   p133
◯ Drinking   p134
◉ Entertainment p135

500 m
0.25 miles

Sights

Fort Siloso
MUSEUM

1 MAP P130, A1

Dating from the 1880s, when Sentosa was called Pulau Blakang Mati (Malay for 'the island behind which lies death'), this British coastal fort was famously useless during the Japanese invasion of 1942. Documentaries, artefacts, animatronics and re-created historical scenes take visitors through the fort's history, and the underground tunnels are fun to explore. The Surrender Chambers bring to life two pivotal moments in Singapore's history: the surrender of the British to the Japanese in 1942, and then the reverse in 1945. (📞6736 8672; www.sentosa.com.sg; Siloso Point, Siloso Rd; admission free; ⏰10am-6pm; 🚻; 🚌Siloso Point; 🚝Siloso Point)

SEA Aquarium
AQUARIUM

2 MAP P130, D1

You'll be gawking at more than 800 species of aquatic creature at Singapore's impressive, sprawling aquarium. The state-of-the-art complex re-creates 49 aquatic habitats found between Southeast Asia, Australia and Africa. The Open Ocean habitat is especially spectacular, its 36m-long, 8.3m-high viewing panel is one of the world's largest. The complex is also home to an interactive, family-friendly exhibition exploring the history of the maritime Silk Route. (📞6577 8888; www.rwsentosa.com; Resorts World, 8 Sentosa Gateway; adult/child under 13yr S$39/29; ⏰10am-7pm; 🅿; 🚝Waterfront)

Images of Singapore Live
MUSEUM

3 MAP P130, C2

Using dramatic light-and-sound effects, actors and immersive exhibitions, Images of Singapore Live resuscitates the nation's history, from humble Malay fishing village to bustling colonial port and beyond. Kids will especially love the Spirit of Singapore Boat Ride, a trippy, high-tech journey that feels just a little *Avatar*. Tickets include entry to Madame Tussauds and are S$10 cheaper when purchased online. (📞6715 4000; www.imagesofsingaporelive.com; 40 Imbiah Rd; adult/child under 13yr S$42/32; ⏰10am-6pm, to 7.30pm Sat & Sun; 🚝Imbiah)

From Here to There

Electric 'beach trams' (buses) run the length of Sentosa's three beaches – Siloso, Palawan and Tanjong – from 9am to 10.30pm Sunday to Friday, and from 9am to midnight Saturday. Two bus routes link the main attractions. Bus A (westbound) and bus B (eastbound) runs 7am to midnight daily. Both routes depart from the bus stop just east of Beach monorail station. The monorail, tram and buses are free.

AJ Hackett Bungy

BUNGEE JUMPING

4 ⊙ MAP P130, C2

The famous New Zealand bungee company has now set up shop on Palawan Beach on Sentosa, complete with a 47m platform to hurtle yourself off should the desire grab you. There's also a giant swing, and a sky bridge for those who'd just like to look. (☑ 6911 3070; www.ajhackett. com; 30 Siloso Beach Walk; bungee S$199, swing S$79, skybridge S$16; ⊙1-7pm, to 8pm Fri-Sun; ☐Siloso Beach)

KidZania

AMUSEMENT PARK

5 ⊙ MAP P130, D2

Young ones get to be the grown-ups in this huge, indoor, kid-sized city. It comprises different 'workplaces', in which kids can try out their dream jobs, from pilot to crime-scene investigator. Parents can only watch, which means waiting around, but it's worth it to see your kid become a firefighter. Weekends are particularly busy. Jobs pay in 'kidZos', which can be used to play or shop within KidZania. (☑1800 653 6888; www.kidzania.com.sg; 01-01/02 Palawan Kidz City, 31 Beach View; adult/child under 18yr S$58/35; ⊙10am-6pm; ☐Beach)

Adventure Cove Waterpark

WATER PARK

6 ⊙ MAP P130, D1

Despite the rides being better suited to kids and families, adult thrill-seekers will appreciate the Riptide Rocket (Southeast Asia's first hydro-magnetic coaster), Pipeline Plunge and Bluwater Bay, a wave pool with serious gusto. (☑6577 8888; www.rwsentosa.com; Resorts World, 8 Sentosa Gateway; adult/child under 13yr S$38/30; ⊙10am-6pm; ☐Waterfront)

iFly

ADVENTURE SPORTS

7 ⊙ MAP P130, C2

If you fancy free-falling from 3660m to 914m without jumping out of a plane, leap into this indoor-skydiving centre. The price includes an hour's instruction followed by a short but thrilling skydive in a vertical wind chamber. Divers must be at least seven years old. Tickets purchased two days in advance for off-peak times are significantly cheaper. See the website for details. (☑6571 0000; www.iflysingapore.com; 43 Siloso Beach Walk; 1/2 skydives S$89/119; ⊙9am-9.30pm, from 11am Wed; ☐Beach)

Skyline Luge Sentosa

ADVENTURE SPORTS

8 ⊙ MAP P130, C2

In the need for speed? Hop onto your luge (think go-cart meets toboggan) and race family and friends around hairpin bends and along bone-shaking straights carved through the forest (mandatory helmets are provided). Young kids will love this. Those with heart conditions or bad backs won't. You'll find entrances at Imbiah Lookout and Siloso. (☑6274 0472; www.skylineluge.com; 45 Siloso Beach Walk; luge & skyride combo from S$24;

⊙10am-9.30pm; 🏖Beach, Imbiah; 🚌Siloso Beach; 🚠Imbiah Lookout, Sentosa Cable Car Station)

Wave House   SURFING

9 ◎ MAP P130, C2

Two specially designed wave pools enable surfer types to practise their gashes and cutbacks at ever-popular Wave House. The non-curling Double Flowrider (one-hour session S$35) is good for beginners, while the 3m FlowBarrel (30-minute session from S$30, closed Tuesdays and Thursdays) is more challenging. Wave House also includes beachside eating and drinking options. (📞6238 1196; www.wavehouse sentosa.com; 36 Siloso Beach Walk; from S$30; ⊙11.30am-9.30pm, from 10.30am Sat & Sun; 🚌Beach)

Eating

Panamericana   GRILL $$

10 🍴 MAP P130, E4

The perfect mix of island casual (minus the sand) and refined service, this bar and grill offers colonial-chic surroundings and sweeping views of the Strait of Singapore. The menu offers a mixture of cuisines found along the Pan-American Hwy, from North America down to Argentina. The empanadas are a must, as is the salt-baked trout with tomatillo verde. (📞6253 8182; www.panamericana.sg; Sentosa Gold Course, 27 Bukit Manis Rd; dishes S$12-50; ⊙noon-11pm Wed-Fri, from 9am Sat & Sun; 🚌B)

Millionaire's Playground

Head down to sleek and sparkly Sentosa Cove in the east of the island and join clued-up locals and expats in this upmarket residential and restaurant precinct. Enjoy your waterside nosh while admiring the stunning marina, jam packed with floating million-dollar play toys of the seriously rich.

Mykonos on the Bay   GREEK $$

11 🍴 MAP P130, F3

At Sentosa Cove, this slick, marina-flanking taverna serves up Hellenic flavours that could make your *papou* weep. Sit alfresco and tuck into perfectly charred, marinated octopus, pan-fried Graviera cheese and house-made *giaourtlou* (spicy lamb sausage). Book ahead if you plan to come later in the week. (📞6334 3818; www.mykonosonthebay.com; 01-10 Quayside Isle, 31 Ocean Way; tapas S$9-26, mains S$26-43; ⊙6-10.30pm Mon-Wed, noon-2.30pm & 6-10.30pm Thu & Fri, noon-10.30pm Sat & Sun; 🚤; 🚌B)

Malaysian Food Street   HAWKER $

With its faux-Malaysian streetscape, this indoor hawker centre near the rotating globe at the entrance to Universal Studios (see 2 ◎ Map p130, D1) feels a bit

Disney. Thankfully, there's nothing fake about the food, cooked by some of Malaysia's best hawker vendors. (www.rwsentosa.com; Level 1, Waterfront, Resorts World, 8 Sentosa Gateway; dishes S$2-11; ⏰11am-9pm, 9am-10pm Fri-Sun; 🚇Waterfront)

Trapizza   PIZZA $$

12 MAP P130, B1

At the quieter end of Siloso Beach, Trapizza is the place to head if you're after a great beach vista coupled with yummy thin-crust pizzas straight from the wood-fire oven. There's also a decent wine and cocktail list, but you may want to stay clear of the pizza-inspired cocktails – pepperoni 'pizzatini', anyone? (📞6376 2662; www.shangri-la.com; Siloso Beach; pizzas S$20-26; ⏰11am-10pm; 🚇Siloso Point)

Brunch at Knolls 🍴

Free-flowing-alcohol Sunday brunch is huge in Singapore, and posh, secluded **Knolls** (Map p130, E3; 📞6591 5046; www.capellahotels.com; Capella, 1 The Knolls; mains S$24-59, Sun brunch from S$148; ⏰7am-11pm; 🚇Imbiah) serves one of the best. Style up and join the see-and-be-seen crowd for scrumptious buffet fare like freshly shucked oysters, sizzling skewers straight from the live grills, fine-cut meats and mountains of cheese.

Drinking

Tanjong Beach Club   BAR

13 🚌 MAP P130, E4

Generally cooler than the bars on Siloso Beach, Tanjong Beach Club is an evocative spot, with loungers on the sand, a small, stylish pool for guests, and a sultry, lounge-and-funk soundtrack. The restaurant serves trendy beachside fare, and a kick-ass weekend-brunch menu. Some of the island's hottest parties happen on this shore; check the website for details. (📞6270 1355; www.tanjongbeachclub.com; 120 Tanjong Beach Walk; ⏰11am-10pm, from 10am Sat, from 9am Sun; 👶; 🚇Tanjong Beach)

FOC Sentosa   BAR

14 🚌 MAP P130, E3

A tiny slice of Barcelona on Palawan Beach, this vibrantly striped hang-out is perfect for lazing the afternoon away either by the compact infinity pool or ensconced on a lounger on the sand. Tummy rumbling? Pick a few bites from the menu of seafood-heavy tapas, and wash it down with a refreshing cocktail – our pick is the 'never ending summer', made with vodka, strawberry and watermelon. (📞6100 1102; www.focsentosa.com; 110 Tanjong Beach Walk; ⏰11.30am-11pm Tue-Sun; 🚇Palawan Beach)

Wings of Time

Coastes
BAR

15  MAP P130, C2

More family-friendly than many of the other beach venues, Coastes has picnic tables on the palm-studded sand and sun loungers (S$22) by the water. Feeling peckish? There's a comprehensive menu of standard offerings, including burgers, pastas, pizzas and salads. (6631 8938; www.coastes.com; 01-05, 50 Siloso Beach Walk; 9am-11pm, to 1am Fri & Sat; Beach; Siloso Beach)

Entertainment

Wings of Time
THEATRE

16 MAP P130, C2

This ambitious show set above the ocean, fuses Lloyd Webber–esque theatricality with an awe-inspiring sound, light and laser extravaganza. Prepare to gasp, swoon and (occasionally) cringe. (6377 9688; www.wingsoftime.com.sg; Siloso Beach; standard/premium seats S$18/23; shows 7.40pm & 8.40pm; Beach)

Explore ◈
Chinatown & the CBD

While Singapore's Chinatown may be a tamer version of its former self, its temples, heritage centre, and booming restaurant and bar scene make the trip there worthwhile. The CBD is best known for its stunning, ever-evolving skyline: rooftop bars jostle with old-school temples, all set against the financial heart that funds Singapore.

The Short List

o **Chinatown Heritage Centre (p138)** *Delving into the unspeakable hardships, destructive temptations and ultimate resilience of the immigrants who gave this part of town its name.*

o **Chinese Theatre Circle (p155)** *Meeting the stars of the show in the unusually informal teahouse.*

o **Ya Kun Kaya Toast (p150)** *Skipping your hotel brekkie for an old-school traditional morning slap-up.*

o **Burnt Ends (p147)** *Giving the chopsticks a rest to savour show-stopping grilled meats at this mod-Oz favourite.*

o **Operation Dagger (p152)** *Chatting and flirting the night away in this basement bar before coming up for air at Club St, the city's bar-scene heartland.*

Getting There & Around

Ⓜ The heart of Chinatown is served by Chinatown MRT station, which spits you out onto Pagoda St. Telok Ayer station is handy for eateries and bars around Amoy St and Club St. Further south, Outram Park and Tanjong Pagar stations are best for Duxton Hill. Raffles Place station is best for the CBD.

Neighbourhood Map on p142

Chinatown market PETER ADAMS/GETTY IMAGES ©

Top Sight 📷
Chinatown Heritage Centre

The Chinatown Heritage Centre lifts the lid off Chinatown's chaotic, colourful and often scandalous past. Its endearing jumble of old photographs, personal anecdotes and re-created environments delivers an evocative stroll through the neighbourhood's highs and lows. Spend some time here and you'll see Chinatown's now tourist-conscious streets in a much more intriguing light.

◉ MAP P142, D2

📞 6224 3928; 48 Pagoda St

www.chinatownheritage centre.com.sg

adult/child under 13yr/7yr S$15/11/free

🕓 9am-8pm, closed 1st Mon of month

Ⓜ Chinatown

Tailor Shop & Living Cubicles

The journey back to old Singapore begins on the ground floor with a re-created tailor shop-front, workshop and cramped living quarters of the tailor's family and apprentices. By the early 1950s, Pagoda St was heaving with tailor shops and this is an incredibly detailed replica of what was once a common neighbourhood fixture.

Re-Created Cubicles

Time travel continues on the 1st floor. Faithfully designed according to the memories and stories of former residents, a row of cubicles will have you peering into the ramshackle living quarters of opium-addicted coolies, stoic Samsui women and even a family of eight! It's a powerful sight, vividly evoking the tough, grim lives that many of the area's residents endured right up to the mid-20th century. Keep your eyes peeled for the vermin (don't worry, they're fake) in every cubicle.

Early Pioneers

The flashy top floor invites you to join the perilous journey Chinese immigrants undertook to reach Singapore, and to discover the customs, cuisine and importance of family networks when they arrived, via a range of sensory exhibits. Many new arrivals fell victim to gambling rings and opium dealers; see the pipes and tiles that they used to lose their minds and their money. One street you won't want to go down is Sago Lane ('Street of the Dead'), where many of Chinatown's poor spent their final days in 'death houses'.

★ Top Tips

o Aim to arrive just after opening – the museum is physically very small so it's best to beat the crowds.

o Allow at least 1½ hours to see and experience all the exhibits, more if you're a history buff.

o Keep your nostrils on alert – you may get a whiff of some old Chinatown smells.

✗ Take a Break

If you arrive before opening time, join the locals at **Nanyang Old Coffee** (☑ 6100 3450; www.nanyangoldcoffee.com; 268 South Bridge Rd; toast sets S$4.30, kopi from S$1.70; ⏰ 7am-10pm) for a traditional breakfast set of *kaya* (coconut jam) toast, runny eggs and *kopi*.

For tasty local fare, head to Chinatown Complex (p148), a labyrinth of hawker stalls. Check the queue at Michelin-starred Hong Kong Soya Sauce Chicken Rice & Noodle (p148) and decide if you can wait.

Walking Tour 🥾

Chinatown Taste Buds & Temples

Given its past as a hotpot of opium dens, death houses and brothels, it's easy to write off today's Chinatown as a paler version of its former self. Yet beyond the tourist tack that chokes Pagoda, Temple and Trengganu Sts lies a still-engrossing neighbourhood where life goes on as it has for generations.

Walk Facts

Start Chinatown Wet Market (M Chinatown)

Finish Telok Ayer St (M Telok Ayer)

Length 1.3km; one to two hours with stops

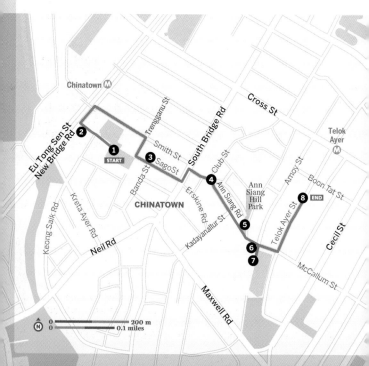

❶ Chinatown Wet Market

Elbow aunties at **Chinatown Wet Market** (Chinatown Complex, 335 Smith St; ⏰5am-noon, stall hours vary), in the basement of the Chinatown Complex. It's a rumble-inducing feast of wriggling seafood, exotic fruits and vegetables, Chinese spices and preserved goods.

❷ Tiong Shian Porridge Centre

Appetite piqued, pull up a plastic stool at **Tiong Shian Porridge Centre** (☎6222 3911; 265 New Bridge Rd; porridge S$3.80-22; ⏰8am-4am), an old-school *kopitiam*. Winners here include delicious porridge with century egg and pork, and the speciality claypot frog-leg porridge.

❸ Chop Tai Chong Kok

Pick up lotus-paste mooncakes at **Chop Tai Chong Kok** (☎6227 5701; www.taichongkok.com; 34 Sago St; pastries from S$1; ⏰9.30am-6pm Mon, to 8pm Tue-Sun), a super-traditional pastry shop in business since 1938. Once known for its sago factories and brothels, Sago St itself now sells everything from barbecued meat to pottery.

❹ Ann Siang Rd & Club St

A quick walk away is trendy Ann Siang Rd, known for its restored heritage terraces and fashionable restaurants, bars and boutiques. Architecture buffs will appreciate the art deco buildings at Nos 15, 17 and 21. Mosey along it and adjacent Club St, also famed for its old shophouses and hip establishments.

❺ Ann Siang Hill Park

At the top of Ann Siang Rd is the entrance to Ann Siang Hill Park. Not only is this Chinatown's highest point, it's a surprising oasis of green. Follow the walkways downward to Amoy St.

❻ Siang Cho Keong Temple

Small Taoist **Siang Cho Keong Temple** (☎6324 4171; 66 Amoy St; admission free; ⏰8am-5pm) was built by the Hokkien community in 1867–69. Left of the temple entrance you'll see a small 'dragon well': drop a coin and make a wish.

❼ Coffee Break

Time for a pit stop at **Coffee Break** (www.facebook.com/coffeebreak amoystreet; 02-78 Amoy Street Food Centre; ⏰7.30am-2.30pm Mon-Fri), a humble drink stall with options like sea-salt caramel lattes and melon milk tea. Make no mistake though, it's still good old Singaporean *kopi* (coffee) – just with a twist.

❽ Telok Ayer St

In Malay, Telok Ayer means 'Water Bay', and Telok Ayer St was a coastal road until land reclamation efforts in the 19th century. Seek out Al-Abrar Mosque, built in the 1850s; Thian Hock Keng Temple, the oldest Hokkien temple in Singapore with a stunning heritage mural on its outside back wall; and Nagore Durgha Shrine, a mosque built between 1828 and 1830 by Chulia Muslims from South India.

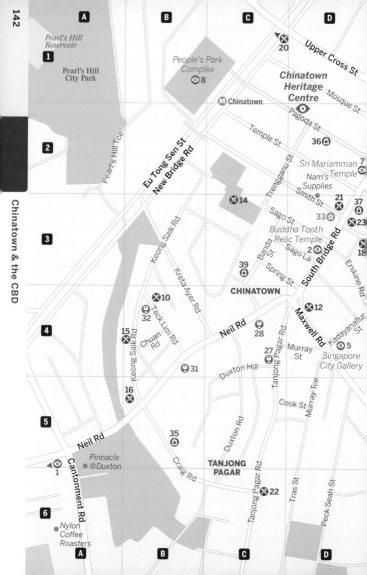

Chinatown & the CBD

A

1 Pearl's Hill Reservoir

Pearl's Hill City Park

B

People's Park Complex
◉ **8**

Ⓜ Chinatown

C

✕ **20**

Upper Cross St

Chinatown Heritage Centre
◉

Pagoda St

Mosque St

D

2

Pearl's Hill Tce

Eu Tong Sen St
New Bridge Rd

Temple St

Trengganu St

36 🔒

Sri Mariamman Temple ◉ **7**

Nam's Supplies

Smith St

Sago St

21
✕

37 🔒

33 ☆

✕ **23**

3

✕ **14**

Buddha Tooth Relic Temple
◉ **2**

Banda St

Sago La

Sago St

South Bridge Rd

Erskine Rd

✕ **18**

39 🔒

Spring St

CHINATOWN

4

Keong Saik Rd

Kreta Ayer Rd

✕ **10**

☕ **32**

Teck Lim Rd

✕ **15**

Chuan Rd

Keong Saik Rd

☕ **28**

Neil Rd

✕ **12**

Maxwell Rd

27

Tanjong Pagar Rd

Murray St

Murray Tce

Kadayanallur St

◉ **5**

Singapore City Gallery

5

☕ **31**

✕ **16**

Duxton Hill

Duxton Rd

Cook St

Neil Rd

Pinnacle ● @Duxton

35 🔒

Craig Rd

TANJONG PAGAR

Duxton Rd

Tanjong Pagar Rd

✕ **22**

Tras St

Peck Seah St

6

◉ **1**
✕

Cantonment Rd

● Nylon Coffee Roasters

A

B

C

D

For reviews see
- Top Sights p138
- Sights p144
- Eating p147
- Drinking p152
- Entertainment p155
- Shopping p156

South Bridge Rd

Hokien St

Nankin St

Chin Chew St

China St

Pekin St

0 — 200 m
0 — 0.1 miles

9 Kenko Wellness Spa

Cross St

Mohamed Ali La

Club St

17

Amoy St

Telok Ayer St

Cecil St

Market St

Robinson Rd

25

Telok Ayer

Cross St

24

Ann Siang Hill

30 38

Ann Siang Rd

Amoy St

Telok Ayer St

Boon Tat St

13

Cross St

Thian Hock Keng Mural

4

Thian Hock Keng Temple

3 6

19

Ann Siang Hill Park

29

Singapore Musical Box Museum

Stanley St

Cecil St

Robinson Rd

Boon Tat St

26

11

McCallum St

Maxwell Link

Telok Ayer St

Cecil St

Robinson Rd

McCallum St

Shenton Way

Telok Ayer Park

Maxwell Rd

Maxwell Link

Shenton Way

34

Sights

Baba House
MUSEUM

1 ◉ MAP P142, A5

Baba House is one of Singapore's best-preserved Peranakan heritage homes. Built in the 1890s, this beautiful blue three-storey building was donated to the National University of Singapore (NUS) by a member of the family that used to live here. The NUS then set about renovating it so that it best matched how it would have looked in 1928 when, according to the family, Baba House was at its most resplendent. The only way in is on a guided/self-guided tour; bookings are essential. Children must be 12 years or older. (☏6227 5731; http://babahouse.nus.edu.sg; 157 Neil Rd; S$10; ⊙1hr tour 10am Tue-Fri, self-guided tour 1.30pm, 2.15pm, 3.15pm & 4pm Sat; MOutram Park)

Buddha Tooth Relic Temple
BUDDHIST TEMPLE

2 ◉ MAP P142, D3

Consecrated in 2008, this hulking, five-storey Buddhist temple is home to what is reputedly a tooth of the Buddha, discovered in a collapsed stupa (Buddhist relic structure) in Mrauk U, Myanmar. While its authenticity is debated, the relic enjoys VIP status inside a 320kg solid-gold stupa in a dazzlingly ornate 4th-floor room. More religious relics await at the 3rd-floor Buddhism museum, while the peaceful rooftop garden

features a huge prayer wheel inside a 10,000 Buddha Pavilion. (☏6220 0220; www.btrts.org.sg; 288 South Bridge Rd; admission free; ⊙7am-7pm, relic viewing 9am-6pm; MChinatown)

Thian Hock Keng Mural
PUBLIC ART

3 ◉ MAP P142, F3

Spanning 44m, this mural, painted by Singaporean artist Yip Yew Chong (accountant by weekday, artist by weekend), tells the story of Singapore's early Hokkien immigrants. You'll find it on the outside rear wall of the Thian Hock Keng Temple start from the right end and follow the immigrants' story, from leaving China to arriving in Singapore, and the sacrifices, hardships and joys they experienced along the way. Discover the mural's hidden secrets via the LocoMole app: instructions are to the mural's far left. (www.yipyc.com; Amoy St, rear wall of Thian Hock Keng Temple, 158 Telok Ayer St; MTelok Ayer)

Thian Hock Keng Temple
TAOIST TEMPLE

4 ◉ MAP P142, F3

Surprisingly, Chinatown's oldest and most important Hokkien temple is often a haven of tranquillity. Built between 1839 and 1842, it's a beautiful place, and was once the favourite landing point of Chinese sailors, before land reclamation pushed the sea far down the road. Typically, the temple's design features are richly

Temple Tales

Before construction of the Thian Hock Keng Temple, the site was home to a much humbler joss house, where Chinese migrants would come to thank Mazu, the goddess of the sea, for their safe arrival. Their donations helped propel construction of the current temple, the low granite barrier of which once served to keep seawater out during high tide. Look up at the temple's ceiling in the right wing and you'll notice a statue of a man, seemingly lifting a beam. The statue is an ode to Indian migrants from nearby Chulia St, who helped construct the building. During restoration works in 1998, one of the roof beams revealed a surprising find – a scroll written by the Qing emperor Guangxu bestowing blessings on Singapore's Chinese community.

Once you're finished inside, make sure to head around to the rear wall on Amoy St. Here you'll discover the detailed Thian Hock Keng Mural by Yip Yew Chong, which depicts the story of Singapore's early Hokkien immigrants.

symbolic: the stone lions at the entrance ward off evil spirits, while the painted depiction of phoenixes and peonies in the central hall symbolise peace and good tidings respectively. (📞6423 4616; www. thianhockkeng.com.sg; 158 Telok Ayer St; admission free; ⏰7.30am-5.30pm; Ⓜ Telok Ayer)

Singapore City Gallery   MUSEUM

5 ◉ MAP P142, D4

See into Singapore's future at this interactive city-planning exhibition, which provides compelling insight into the government's resolute policies of land reclamation, high-rise housing and meticulous urban planning. At the time of research, the gallery was closed for a revamp;

however, a number of temporary exhibits and the island-wide model remain available for viewing. The main gallery is due to reopen 2019. (📞6321 8321; www. ura.gov.sg/citygallery; URA Centre, 45 Maxwell Rd; admission free; ⏰9am-5pm Mon-Sat; Ⓜ Chinatown, Tanjong Pagar)

Singapore Musical Box Museum   MUSEUM

6 ◉ MAP P142, F4

Walk through music history and be captivated by the exquisite melodies of these antique music boxes, some more than 200 years old. Peer into the inner workings of the very first, and rather basic, boxes all the way through to cupboard-sized, multi-instrument music makers. One was even

Public Housing Panorama

For killer city views at a bargain S$6, head to the 50th-floor rooftop of **Pinnacle@Duxton** (Map p142, A5; 🗹8683 7760; www.pinnacle duxton.com.sg; Block 1G, 1 Cantonment Rd; ◷9am-9pm; MOutram Park), the world's largest public housing complex. Skybridges connecting the seven towers provide a 360-degree sweep of city, port and sea. Chilling out is encouraged, with patches of lawn, modular furniture and sun loungers. Find the 'blink or you'll miss it' ticket booth at level one, Block G, hand over your cash and register your Ez-Link transport card, before taking the lift up to the 50th floor, where you'll tap your card at the gate – stand inside the turnstile before tapping.

destined for the *Titanic* but missed the boat! There's something for everyone; the older generations will love the old-time tunes, and youngsters will marvel at what the first iPod looked like. (🗹6221 0102; www.singaporemusicalboxmuseum. org; 168 Telok Ayer St; 40min tour per person S$12, child under 6yr free; ◷10am-6pm Wed-Mon, tours run hourly from 10am-5pm; MTelok Ayer)

Sri Mariamman Temple

HINDU TEMPLE

7 ◉ MAP P142, D2

Paradoxically in the middle of Chinatown, this is the oldest Hindu temple in Singapore, originally built in 1823, then rebuilt in 1843. You can't miss the fabulously animated, Technicolor 1930s *gopuram* (tower) above the entrance, the key to the temple's South Indian Dravidian style. Sacred-cow sculptures grace the boundary walls, while the *gopuram* is covered in kitsch

plasterwork images of Brahma the creator, Vishnu the preserver and Shiva the destroyer. (🗹6223 4064; www.smt.org.sg; 244 South Bridge Rd; take photos/videos S$3/6; ◷5.30am-noon & 6-9pm; MChinatown)

People's Park Complex

MASSAGE

8 ◉ MAP P142, B1

Heady with the scent of Tiger balm, Singapore's oldest mall is well known for its cheap massage joints. Our favourite is **Mr Lim Foot Reflexology** (🗹6327 4498; 20min foot reflexology S$10; ◷10.30am-10pm), where you'll queue with regulars awaiting a robust rubdown. Feeling adventurous? Try one of the fish-pond foot spas, where schools of fish nibble the dead skin right off your feet. (www.peoplesparkcomplex.sg; 1 Park Cres; ◷9am-10pm, shop hours vary; MChinatown)

Kenko Wellness Spa
SPA

9  MAP P142, E2

Kenko is the McDonald's of Singapore's spas with branches throughout the city, but there's nothing drive-through about its foot reflexology and forceful Kenko massage (choose the Swedish massage for softer pressure). (📞6223 0303; www.kenko.com.sg; 199 South Bridge Rd; reflexology per 40min S$59, body massage per 60min S$120; ⏰10am-10.30pm; ⓂChinatown)

Eating

Burnt Ends
BARBECUE $$$

10 ✖ MAP P142, B4

The best seats at this mod-Oz hot spot are at the counter, which offers a prime view of chef Dave Pynt and his 4-tonne, wood-fired ovens and custom grills. The affable Aussie cut his teeth under Spanish charcoal deity Victor Arguinzoniz (Asador Etxebarri), an education echoed in pulled pork shoulder in homemade brioche, and beef marmalade and pickles on chargrilled sourdough. (📞6224 3933; www.burntends.com.sg; 20 Teck Lim Rd; dishes S$8-45; ⏰6-11pm Tue-Thu, 11.45am-2pm & 6-11pm Fri & Sat; ⓂChinatown, Outram Park)

A Noodle Story
NOODLES $$

11 ✖ MAP P142, F4

With a snaking line and proffered apology that 'we may sell out earlier than stipulated timing' on the facade, this one-dish-only stall is a magnet for Singapore

Pinnacle@Duxton

foodies. The object of desire is Singapore–style ramen created by two young chefs, Gwern Khoo and Ben Tham. It's Japanese ramen meets won-ton mee (noodles): pure bliss in a bowl topped with a crispy potato-wrapped prawn. (☏ 9027 6289; www.anoodlestorydot-com.wordpress.com; 01-39 Amoy Street Food Centre, cnr Amoy & Telok Ayer Sts; noodles S$8-15; ⏰ 11.15am-2.30pm & 5.30-7.30pm Mon-Fri, 10.30am-1.30pm Sat; Ⓜ Telok Ayer)

Maxwell Food Centre HAWKER $

12 ✖ MAP P142, D4

One of Chinatown's most accessible hawker centres, Maxwell is a solid spot to savour some of the city's street-food staples. While stalls slip in and out of favour with Singapore's fickle diners, enduring favourites include **Tian Tian Hainanese Chicken Rice** (chicken rice from S$3.50; ⏰ 10am-8pm Tue-Sun) and **Rojak, Popiah & Cockle** (popiah S$1.50, rojak S$3-8; ⏰ 10am-10pm), as well as new favourite **Lad & Dad** (☏ 9247 7385; www.facebook.com/ladanddadsg; dishes S$4-12; ⏰ 11.30am-2.30pm & 5.30-9pm Mon-Fri) serving British fare. (cnr Maxwell & South Bridge Rds; dishes S$2.50-12; ⏰ 8am-2am, stall hours vary; 🖋; Ⓜ Chinatown)

Cheek By Jowl AUSTRALIAN $$$

13 ✖ MAP P142, G3

The gleaming open kitchen sets the stage for chef Rishi Naleendra to create his seasonal modern Australian masterpieces – bar seats offer a front-row view. The menu is short, but when you realise you'd like to order everything you'll be glad the options are limited. If available the 'raw beef salad' with Brussels sprouts and macadamia shouldn't be missed. (☏ 6221 1911; www.cheekbyjowl.com.sg; 21 Boon Tat St; à la carte lunch 2/3/5 courses S$42/48/68, à la carte dinner (Mon-Thu) 3 courses S$88, chef's menu 5/7 courses S$98/118; ⏰ noon-2pm & 6-10pm Mon-Fri, 6-10pm Sat; Ⓜ Telok Ayer)

Chinatown Complex HAWKER $

14 ✖ MAP P142, C3

Leave Smith St's revamped 'Chinatown Food Street' to the out-of-towners and join old-timers and foodies at this nearby labyrinth, now home to Michelin-starred **Hong Kong Soya Sauce Chicken Rice & Noodle** (Hawker Chan Soya Sauce Chicken Rice & Noodle; www.facebook.com/hawkerchan; dishes S$2-3; ⏰ 10.30am-3.30pm Thu-Tue). You decide if the two-hour wait is worth it. Other standouts include mixed claypot rice at **Lian He Ben Ji Claypot Rice** (☏ 6227 2470; dishes S$2.50-5, claypot rice S$5-20; ⏰ 4.30-10.30pm Fri-Wed) and the rich, nutty satay at **Shi Xiang Satay** (10 sticks S$6; ⏰ 4-9pm Fri-Wed). (335 Smith St; dishes from S$1.50). (stall hours vary; Ⓜ Chinatown)

Butcher Boy FUSION $$$

15 ✖ MAP P142, B4

Meat lovers will relish the Asian-inspired creations by chef-owner

Hawker Centre 101

Fragrant chicken rice, nutty satay, sweet and sour *rojak* (salad), spicy barbecue sambal stingray: Singapore's hawker food is the stuff of legend, and celebrity chefs, including the late Anthony Bourdain and *New York Times* writer Johnny Apple, have raved about the dazzling array of cheap, lip-smacking dishes available. There's really no better way to get into Singapore's psyche than through its cuisine, so roll up your sleeves, follow these instructions, and get ready to sweat it out over steaming plates of tried, tested and perfected local favourites.

o Bag a seat first, especially if it's busy. Sit a member of your group at a table, or 'chope' (save) your seat by laying a packet of tissues there. Don't worry if there are no completely free tables; it's normal to share with strangers.

o If there's a table number, note it as the stall owner uses it as a reference for food delivery.

o If the stall has a self-service sign, you'll have to carry the food to the table yourself. Otherwise, the vendor brings your order to you.

o Ignore wandering touts who try to sit you down and plonk menus in front of you.

o It's customary to return your tray when finished, although there are a few roaming cleaners who'll take your empty dishes.

Andrew Walsh, formerly of tapas haven **Esquina** (☎6222 1616; www.esquina.com.sg), in this dimly lit shophouse grill and bar. Perfectly charred, the tender black Angus rib eye is not to be missed, and the masala roasted cauliflower has vegetarians swooning. The good vibes keep on rolling with wickedly strong cocktails.

Happy hour runs 5pm to 7pm daily and the bar seating is great for solo drinkers and diners. (☎6221 6833; www.butcherboy.com.sg; 31 Keong Saik Rd; mains S$24-42;

⊙noon-3pm Wed, Thu & Fri, 6-10.30pm Sun-Thu, to 11pm Fri & Sat, bar 5pm-late; MChinatown, Outram Park)

Neon Pigeon JAPANESE $$$

16 ✖ MAP P142, B5

Join the crowd at this graffiti-pimped, cocktail-swilling izakaya for produce-driven, finger-licking Japanese sharing plates. Peck your beak at winners like fluffy soft-shell-crab bao with corn, avocado and black pepper teriyaki; moreish edamame Tokyo hummus with curry chips; and smoky baby back ribs with sake barbecue sauce. Six small dishes between two should suffice. The cocktail list is definitely worth sampling. (📞 6222 3623; www.neonpigeonsg.com; 1A Keong Saik Rd; small dishes S$9-19, large dishes S$16-48; ⏰ 6pm-midnight Mon-Sat; 🛜; Ⓜ Outram Park, Chinatown)

Ya Kun Kaya Toast   CAFE $

17 ❌ MAP P142, F2

Though it's now part of a chain, this airy, retro coffeeshop is an institution, and the best way to start the day the Singaporean way. The speciality is buttery *kaya* toast, dipped in runny eggs (add white pepper and a swirl of soy sauce) and washed down with strong *kopi*. Enjoy a giggle at the Singaporean humour posters. (📞 6438 3638; www.yakun.com; 01-01 Far East Sq, 18 China St; kaya toast set S$4.80, kopi S$1.80; ⏰ 7.30am-7pm Mon-Fri, to 4.30pm Sat, 8.30am-3pm Sun; Ⓜ Telok Ayer)

Coconut Club   MALAYSIAN $$

18 ❌ MAP P142, D3

Not just any old nasi lemak joint, here they're nuts about coconuts and only a certain Malaysian West African (MAWA) hybrid will do. Chicken is super crispy, encrusted in a flavour-punching lemongrass, ginger and galangal coating. The sambal (sauce of fried chilli, onions and prawn paste), however, is on the mild side. Save room for the refreshing *cendol* dessert. (📞 6635 2999;

www.thecoconutclub.sg; 6 Ann Siang Hill; mains S$12.80; ⏰ 11am-3pm & 6-9.30pm Mon-Sat, 11am-3pm Sun; Ⓜ Chinatown, Telok Ayer)

Lau Pa Sat   HAWKER $

19 ❌ MAP P142, H4

Lau Pa Sat means 'Old Market' in Hokkien, which is appropriate as the handsome iron structure shipped out from Glasgow in 1894 remains intact. It's a favourite spot for CBD workers, who flock here for hawker favourites like fishball noodles and chicken rice. In the evening, the facing Boon Tat St transforms into **Satay Street** (satay sticks around S$0.70; ⏰ 7pm-1am Mon-Fri, 3pm-1am Sat & Sun), the famous eating spot. (www.laupasat.biz; 18 Raffles Quay; dishes from S$4; ⏰ 24hr, stall hours vary; Ⓜ Telok Ayer, Raffles Place)

Red Star   CHINESE $$

20 ❌ MAP P142, C1

Armed with trolley-clutching aunties who swoop like fighter jets, classic Red Star is perfect for a Hong Kong–style yum cha. Keep your ears pricked for the pork bao and *liu sha* bao, the latter a smooth bun filled with runny salted egg-yolk custard. The restaurant is tucked away on the 7th floor of a HDB block; look for red signs. (📞 6532 5266; www.redstarrestaurant.com.sg; Level 7, 54 Chin Swee Rd; yum cha from S$3.50-8; ⏰ yum cha 8am-3pm Mon-Sat, from 7am Sun, dinner 6-10pm Mon-Sat; Ⓜ Chinatown)

Ci Yan Organic Vegetarian Health Food
VEGETARIAN $

21 MAP P142, D3

Excellent food, a very friendly manager and an informal atmosphere make this a fine choice for a no-fuss vegetarian meal in the heart of Chinatown. It tends to only have five or six dishes (when we ate here choices ranged from the delicious brown-rice set meal to minestrone soup, vegetarian Penang laksa and almond tofu), written up on a blackboard daily. (6225 9026; www.facebook.com/ciyanveg; 8-10 Smith St; mains S$4-9; noon-10pm; ; Chinatown)

Ginza Tendon Itsuki
JAPANESE $$

22 MAP P142, C6

Life's few certainties include taxes, death and a queue outside this dedicated *tendon* (tempura served on rice) eatery. Patience is rewarded with cries of *irrashaimase!* (welcome) and generous bowls of Japanese comfort grub. Both the tempura and rice are cooked to perfection, drizzled in sweet and sticky soy sauce, and served with *chawanmushi* (Japanese egg custard), miso soup and pickled vegetables. A cash-only bargain. (6221 6678; www.tendonitsuki.sg; 101 Tanjong Pagar Rd; mains S$13-14; 11.30am-2.30pm & 5.30-10pm; ; Tanjong Pagar)

Ya Kun Kaya Toast

Tong Heng

BAKERY **$**

23 MAP P142, D3

Hit the spot at this veteran pastry shop, specialising in pastries, tarts and cakes from the southern Chinese province of Guangdong. While locals rightfully flock here for the melt-in-your-mouth diamond shaped egg tarts, leave room for the slightly charred perfection of the char siew su (barbecue pork puff). Addictive personalities beware. (📞6223 3649; www.tongheng.com. sg; 285 South Bridge Rd; snacks from S$1.70; ⏰9am-9pm; MChinatown)

Drinking

Operation Dagger

COCKTAIL BAR

24 🍺 MAP P142, E3

From the cloud-like light sculpture to the boundary-pushing cocktails, extraordinary is the keyword here. To encourage experimentation, drinks are described by flavour, not spirit, the latter shelved in uniform apothecary-like bottles. Sample the sesame-infused Gomashio or the textural surprise of the Hot & Cold. Head up the hill where Club St and Ann Siang Hill meet; a symbol shows the way. (📞6438 4057; www.operationdagger.com; 7 Ann Siang Hill; ⏰6pm-late Tue-Sat; MChinatown, Telok Ayer)

Employees Only

COCKTAIL BAR

25 🍺 MAP P142, F2

This outpost of the famous New York cocktail bar of the same name has brought a slice of big-city buzz to Singapore, along with a dazzling array of innovative drinks. Some of the sting from the eye-watering prices is soothed by the free-pour mixing method; lightweights may be knocked from their perch. A pink neon 'psychic' sign marks the entrance. (http://employeesonlysg. com; 112 Amoy St; ⏰5pm-1am Mon-Fri, to 2am Sat, 6pm-1am Sun; MTelok Ayer)

HDB Caffeine Hit

The ground-floor space of Singapore's public housing blocks (HDBs) are usually scattered with gossipy uncles and aunties and shrieking kids. At Everton Park, however, you're just as likely to find third-wave coffee geeks. The HDB complex is home to **Nylon Coffee Roasters** (Map p142, A6; 📞6220 2330; www.nyloncoffee.sg; 01-40, 4 Everton Park; ⏰8.30am-5.30pm Mon & Wed-Fri, 9am-6pm Sat & Sun; MOutram Park, Tanjong Pagar), a standing-room-only cafe-roastery helmed by a personable, gung-ho crew of coffee fanatics, chatting away with customers about their latest coffee-sourcing trip abroad (they deal directly with the farmers). Everton Park is 500m south of Outram Park MRT. Enter from Cantonment Rd, directly opposite the seven-tower Pinnacle@Duxton (p146).

Native
BAR

26 MAP P142, F4

This hidden bar, in hot-spot-heavy Amoy St, is the brainchild of bartender extraordinaire Vijay Mudaliar (formerly of Operation Dagger (p152)), and his concoctions have everyone talking. With spirits sourced from around the region – such as Thai rum and Sri Lankan arak, paired with locally foraged ingredients – expect the unexpected. (☑8869 6520; www.tribenative.com; 52A Amoy St; ☺6pm-midnight Mon-Sat; Ⓜ Telok Ayer)

Tippling Club
COCKTAIL BAR

27 MAP P142, C4

Tippling Club propels mixology to dizzying heights, with a technique and creativity that could turn a teetotaller into a born-again soak. Sample the Dreams & Desires menu before ordering by chewing your way through alcohol-infused gummy bears, which give a hint of what's to come. Our pick is the champagne-based Beauty, served with a cherry sorbet lipstick. (☑6475 2217; www.tipplingclub.com; 38 Tanjong Pagar Rd; ☺noon-midnight Mon-Fri, from 6pm Sat; Ⓜ Tanjong Pagar)

Tea Chapter
TEAHOUSE

28 MAP P142, C4

Queen Elizabeth and Prince Philip dropped by this tranquil teahouse in 1989, and for S$10 you can sit at the table they sipped at. A minimum charge of S$8 per person will

Beer Hawkers

Clink craft-beer glasses with locals at the Chinatown Complex (p148), where a few fancy beer hawkers such as Smith Street Taps (p154) and have opened their shutters right next to some of the best eats in town – the satays from nearby Shi Xiang Satay (p148) complement the suds perfectly. Don't be put off if the centre looks closed when you enter; check the map at the top of the escalator to find the stalls and join the party.

get you a heavenly pot of loose-leaf tea, prepared with traditional precision. The selection is excellent and the adjoining shop sells tea and a selection of beautiful tea sets.

Want to take your tea tasting to a new level? Book a tea appreciation package (from S$70 for two persons), either the 'fragrance and aroma' or 'shades of tea', and become a tea master. (☑6226 1175; www.teachapter.com; 9-11 Neil Rd; ☺teahouse 11am-9pm Sun-Thu, to 10.30pm Fri & Sat, shop 10.30am-9pm Sun-Thu, to 10.30pm Fri & Sat; Ⓜ Chinatown)

Spiffy Dapper
COCKTAIL BAR

29 MAP P142, E4

Keep your eyes peeled for the Dapper Coffee sign and then quick, before anyone sees, scuttle up the stairs and through the engraved doors. Choose from the list of classic cocktails or let the bar tenders do their thing – gin lovers, you're in for a treat as the collection here is legendary. (☎8742 8908; www.spiffydapper.com; 73 Amoy St; ⏰5pm-late Mon-Fri, from 6pm Sat & Sun; Ⓜ Telok Ayer)

Screening Room Rooftop Bar

BAR

30 Ⓣ MAP P142, E3

Perched atop a mini cinema, **Screening Room** (☎6532 3357; S$15; ⏰screenings 7pm & 9.30pm Mon-Thu, 8.30pm Fri & Sat), this rooftop bar is a mix of arresting city views, tipsy expats and knockout cocktails. For audible conversation, head up early in the night or earlier in the week. If crowds and a buzzing vibe are your thing, Friday and Saturday nights will have you purring. To reserve a table, call or book via its website two days ahead. (☎6221 2694; www.screeningroom.com.sg; 12 Ann Siang Rd; ⏰5.30pm-2am Mon-Thu, to 3am Fri, to 4am Sat; Ⓜ Chinatown, Telok Ayer)

Smith Street Taps

CRAFT BEER

Head to this hawker-centre stall in the Chinatown Complex (see **14** Ⓧ Map p142, C3) for a top selection of ever-changing craft and premium draught beers from around the world. A few food stalls stay open around this back section of the hawkers market, creating a local hidden-bar buzz. Tuck into a plate of smoky skewers from Shi Xiang Satay (p148) with your brew. Last call 15 minutes before closing.

Sister stall the **Good Beer Company** (02-58 Chinatown Complex; ⏰6.30-10.30pm Mon-Sat) sells bottled suds. (☎9430 2750; www.facebook.com/smithstreettaps; 02-62 Chinatown Complex, 335 Smith St; ⏰6.30-10.30pm Tue-Thu, 5-11pm Fri, 2-10.30pm Sat; Ⓜ Chinatown)

Taboo

CLUB, LGBT

31 Ⓣ MAP P142, B4

Conquer the dance floor at what remains the favourite gay club in town. Expect the requisite line-up of shirtless gyrators, doting straight women and regular racy-themed nights. The dance floor goes ballistic from midnight and the beats bump till the wee hours of the morning. (☎6225 6256; www.taboo.sg; 65 Neil Rd; ⏰8pm-2am Wed & Thu, 10pm-3am Fri, to 4am Sat; Ⓜ Outram Park, Chinatown)

Potato Head Singapore

COCKTAIL BAR

32 Ⓣ MAP P142, B4

Offshoot of the legendary Bali bar, this standout, multi-level playground incorporates three spaces, all reached via a chequered stairwell embellished with creepy storybook murals and giant glowing dolls. Skip the Three Buns burger joint and head straight for the dark, plush glamour of cocktail lounge Studio 1939 or the laid-back frivolity of the rooftop tiki bar. (☎6327 1939; www.ptthead.com; 36 Keong Saik Rd; ⏰Studio 1939 & rooftop bar 5pm-late; 🛜; Ⓜ Outram Park)

Entertainment

Chinese Theatre Circle OPERA

33 ⭐ MAP P142, D3

Teahouse evenings organised by this nonprofit opera company are a wonderful, informal introduction to Chinese opera. Every Friday and Saturday at 8pm there is a brief talk on Chinese opera, followed by a 45-minute excerpt from an opera classic, performed by actors in full costume. You can also opt for a pre-show Chinese meal at 7pm. Book ahead. (📞6323 4862; www.ctcopera.com; 5 Smith St; show & snacks S$25, show & dinner S$40; ⏰7-9pm Fri & Sat; Ⓜ Chinatown)

Singapore Chinese Orchestra CLASSICAL MUSIC

34 ⭐ MAP P142, G6

Using traditional instruments such as the *liuqin, ruan* and *sanxian,* the SCO treats listeners to classical Chinese concerts throughout the year. Concerts are held at the SCO Concert Hall as well as at various venues around the city, with occasional collaborations showcasing jazz musicians. Tickets can be purchased via SISTIC (p49) or at the on-site box office. Check the website for upcoming performances. (SCO; 📞6557 4034; www.sco.com.sg; Singapore Conference Hall, 7 Shenton Way; ⏰box office 10am-6.45pm Mon-Fri, 6-9pm SCO concert nights; Ⓜ Tanjong Pagar, Downtown)

Potato Head Singapore

Paper, Death & Sago Lane

The curious paper objects on sale around Chinatown – from miniature cars to computers – are offerings burned at funeral wakes to ensure the material wealth of the dead. Veteran **Nam's Supplies** (Map p142, D3; ☑6324 5872; www.facebook.com/namssupplies; 22 Smith St; ⏰8am-7pm; Ⓜ Chinatown) has been peddling such offerings since 1948, when nearby Sago Lane heaved with so-called 'death houses', where the dying spent their final days.

Shopping

Tong Mern Sern Antiques ANTIQUES

35 🔒 MAP P142, B5

An Aladdin's cave of dusty furniture, books, records, wood carvings, porcelain, and other bits and bobs, Tong Mern Sern is a curious hunting ground for Singapore nostalgia. A banner hung above the front door proclaims: 'We buy junk and sell antiques. Some fools buy. Some fools sell'. Better have your wits about you. (☑6223 1037; www.tmsantiques.com; 51 Craig Rd; ⏰9.30am-5.30pm Mon-Sat, from 1.30pm Sun; Ⓜ Outram Park)

Anthony the Spice Maker SPICES

If you want to re-create the aromas and tastes of Singapore at home, head to this tiny stall in the Chinatown Complex (see 14 ✖ Map p142, C3) where little brown airtight packets, which don't allow even the slightest whiff of the heady spices to escape, are uniformly lined up. Anthony is only too happy to help you choose, but we can personally recommend the meat *rendang* blend. (☑9117 7573; www.anthonythespicemaker.com; B1-169 Chinatown Complex, 335 Smith St; ⏰8.15am-3.30pm Tue-Sun; Ⓜ Chinatown)

East Inspirations ANTIQUES

36 🔒 MAP P142, D2

East Inspirations is jam-packed with antique figurines, trinkets and some furniture. Look out for the beautifully embroidered Chinese Manchu wedding shoes. There's a second outlet at 233 South Bridge Rd. (☑6224 2993; www.east-inspirations.com; 33 Pagoda St; ⏰10.30am-6.30pm; Ⓜ Chinatown)

Eu Yan Sang HEALTH & WELLNESS

37 🔒 MAP P142, D3

Get your *qi* back in order at Singapore's most famous and user-friendly Chinese medicine store. Pick up some Monkey Bezoar powder to relieve excess phlegm, or Liu Jun Zi pills to dispel dampness. You'll find herbal teas, soups and oils, and you can even consult a practitioner of Chinese medicine at the clinic next door (bring your

Anthony the Spice Maker

passport). (☎6223 6333; www.
euyansang.com.sg; 269 South Bridge
Rd; ⏰shop 9am-6.30pm Mon-Sat,
clinic 8.30am-6pm Mon-Tue & Thu-Fri,
from 9am Wed, 8.30am-7.30pm Sat;
Ⓜ Chinatown)

innit
FASHION & ACCESSORIES

38 🔒 MAP P142, E3

Singaporean fashionistas swoon
over the flowing fabrics and perfect pleating of Thai fashion house
innit. Pieces are easily mixed and
matched, and the high quality
means you'll get plenty of wear
from each item. (☎9781 7496; www.
innitbangkok.com; 13 Ann Siang Hill;
⏰11am-8pm Wed-Sat; Ⓜ Chinatown,
Telok Ayer)

Hear Records
MUSIC

39 🔒 MAP P142, C3

Rack upon rack of wooden boxes
filled with music gold awaits
those who like to flick at this
vinyl-lovers paradise. Tucked
at the end of a block near the
Buddha Tooth Relic Temple, this
bright-orange-painted store, with
fun black-and-white 'sleeveface'
picture wall, stocks new and used
vinyl in pretty much every genre.
(☎6221 3221; www.facebook.com/
hearrecordschinatown; 01-98, Block
5, Banda St; ⏰11am-7.30pm Mon-Sat,
noon-6pm Sun; Ⓜ Chinatown)

Walking Tour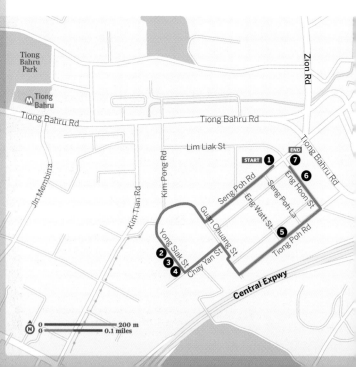

A Lazy Morning in Tiong Bahru

Spend a late weekend morning in Tiong Bahru, three stops from Raffles Place on the East–West (green) MRT line. More than just hip boutiques, bars and cafes, this low-rise neighbourhood was Singapore's first public-housing estate, and its walk-up, art-deco apartments now make for unexpected architectural treats.

Walk Facts

Start Tiong Bahru Market (Ⓜ Tiong Bahru)

Finish We Need A Hero (Ⓜ Tiong Bahru)

Length 1.5km; one to two hours

❶ Tiong Bahru Market

Whet your appetite exploring the wet market at the **Tiong Bahru Market & Food Centre** (83 Seng Poh Rd; dishes from S$3; ⏲6am-late, stall hours vary), then head upstairs to the hawker centre for *shui kueh* (steamed rice cake with diced preserved radish) at **Jian Bo Shui Kueh** (www.jianboshuikueh.com; 02-05 Tiong Bahru Market & Food Centre, 5 shui kueh S$2.50; ⏲5.30am-10pm).

❷ Book Hunting

BooksActually (☎6222 9195; www.booksactually.com; 9 Yong Siak St; ⏲10am-8pm Tue-Sat, to 6pm Mon & Sun) is one of Singapore's coolest independent bookshops, with often unexpected choices of fiction and non-fiction. For beautiful children's books, check out **Woods in the Books** (☎6222 9980; www.woodsinthebooks.sg; ⏲10am-7pm Tue-Fri, to 8pm Sat, to 6pm Sun), three doors down.

❸ Nana & Bird

Originally a pop-up concept store, **Nana & Bird** (www.nanaandbird.com; 1M Yong Siak St; ⏲noon-7pm Mon-Fri, from 11am Sat & Sun) is a sound spot for fresh independent fashion and accessories for women, with labels including Singapore designers Aijek and Rye.

❹ Plain Vanilla Bakery

If your idea of heaven involves frosted icing, head to **Plain Vanilla Bakery** (☎8363 7614; www.plainvanillabakery.com; 1D Yong Siak St; cupcakes from S$4.20; ⏲8am-7pm Mon-Sat, 9am-6pm Sun). The passion project of ex-lawyer-turned-baker Vanessa Kenchington, this bakery-cafe peddles ridiculously scrumptious cupcakes in flavours such as Earl Grey lavender.

❺ Ah Chiang's

Join old-timers and Gen-Y nostalgics for a little Cantonese soul food at **Ah Chiang's** (☎6557 0084; www.facebook.com/ahchiangporridgesg; 01-38, 65 Tiong Poh Rd; porridge S$5-6; ⏲6am-11pm). The star turn at this retro corner *kopitiam* (coffeeshop) is fragrant, charcoal-fired congee.

❻ Tiong Bahru Bakery

The quintessential Frenchman, baker Gontran Cherrier has all and sundry itching for a little French lovin' at **Tiong Bahru Bakery** (☎6220 3430; www.tiongbahrubakery.com; 01-70, 56 Eng Hoon St; pastries S$2.20-4.60, sandwiches S$5.30-12; ⏲8am-8pm). Faultless pastries include flaky *kouign amanns* (Breton-style pastry); perfect with luscious coffee from Common Man Coffee Roasters.

❼ We Need a Hero

Especially for blokes, **We Need A Hero** (☎6222 5590; www.weneedahero.sg; 01-86, 57 Eng Hoon St; barber cut from S$60, shave from S$35; ⏲11am-9pm Mon-Fri, from 10am Sat, 10am-8pm Sun) is the perfect place to plonk yourself down and let the Hero team unleash their grooming superpowers – you'll be slick in no time.

Walking Tour 🥾

Geylang

Contradiction thrives in Geylang, a neighbourhood as famous for its shrines, temples and mosques as for its brothels and back-alley gambling dens. Catch the East–West (green) MRT line four stops from Raffles Place and spend the afternoon wandering quaint lorongs (alleys) and religious buildings, before heading back to neon-lit Geylang Rd for a lively evening of people-watching and lip-smacking local grub.

Walk Facts

Start Geylang Lor 9 Fresh Frog Porridge (Ⓜ Kallang/Aljunied)

Finish Rochor Beancurd (Ⓜ Paya Lebar)

Length 3km; two to four hours

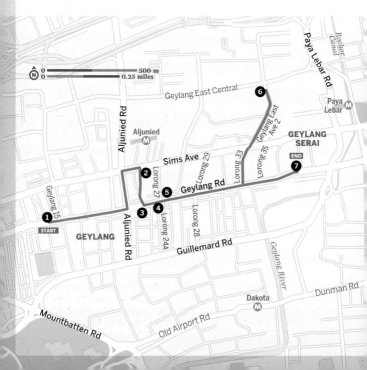

❶ Geylang Lor 9 Fresh Frog Porridge

Geylang is famous for its frog porridge and the best place to try it is **Geylang Lor 9 Fresh Frog Porridge** (235 Geylang Rd; frog porridge from S$8.50; ⏱3pm-3.30am). Its Cantonese-style version is beautifully smooth and gooey, and only live frogs are used, so the meat is always fresh.

❷ Amitabha Buddhist Centre

Take a class on dharma and meditation at the **Amitabha Buddhist Centre** (☎6745 8547; www.fpmtabc.org; 44 Lorong 25A; ⏱10.30am-6pm Tue-Sat, from 10am Sun); its upstairs meditation hall is open to the public and filled with devotional objects. Check the website for class schedules.

❸ No Signboard Seafood

Get messy over white-pepper crab at **No Signboard Seafood** (☎6842 3415; www.nosignboardseafood.com; 414 Geylang Rd; dishes S$15-60, crab per kg from S$80; ⏱11am-1am). Madam Ong Kim Hoi started out with an unnamed hawker stall (hence 'No Signboard'), but the popularity of her seafood made her a rich woman, with four restaurants.

❹ Lorong 24A

One alley worth strolling down is **Lorong 24A**, lined with renovated shophouses from which the sounds of chanting emerge.

Many have been taken over by the numerous small Buddhist associations in the area. Close by, tree-lined Lorong 27 is jammed with colourful shrines and temples.

❺ Geylang Thian Huat Siang Joss Paper

Old-school **Geylang Thian Huat Siang Joss Paper** (503 Geylang Rd; ⏱8am-9.30pm) sells paper offerings used at funeral wakes. You'll find everything from giant cash registers to lifelike shoes and piles of cash, all thrown into the fire to ensure a comfortable afterlife.

❻ Sri Sivan Temple

Built on Orchard Rd in the 1850s, the whimsically ornate **Sri Sivan Temple** (☎6743 4566; www.sst.org.sg; 24 Geylang East Ave 2; admission free; ⏱6am-noon & 6-9pm) was uprooted and moved to Serangoon Rd in the 1980s before moving to its current location in 1993. The Hindu temple is unique for its fusion of North and South Indian architectural influences.

❼ Rochor Beancurd

End on a sweet note at tiny **Rochor Beancurd** (☎6748 3989; www.rochorbeancurdhouse.wix.com/home; 745 Geylang Rd; dough sticks S$1.20, bean curd from S$1.60; ⏱24hr; ✍). People head here from all over the city for a bowl of silky bean curd (opt for it warm). Order a side of dough sticks and dip to your heart's content. Oh, and did we mention the egg tarts?

Explore

Joo Chiat (Katong)

This picturesque neighbourhood of restored multicoloured shophouses has, in recent years, become known as the spiritual heartland of Singapore's Peranakan culture. Spend a few hours wandering the ornate shophouse-lined streets ducking in and out of heritage temples, dusty antiques workshops, Islamic fashion boutiques, low-fuss eateries and trendy cafes. Complete your day with a trip to breezy East Coast Park.

The Short List

○ **Peranakan Terrace Houses (p167)** *Eyeing-up the exuberant architectural candy of Joo Chiat and Koon Seng Rds.*

○ **328 Katong Laksa (p168)** *Licking to the bottom of the bowl at this cult-status laksa shop.*

○ **Katong Antique House (p165)** *Delving into rich Peranakan culture.*

○ **East Coast Park (p167)** *Riding a bicycle or roller-blading along East Coast Park before plonking yourself down to rest, watch the ships in the strait and soak up the atmosphere.*

Getting There & Around

Ⓜ Paya Lebar takes you to the north end of Joo Chiat Rd.

🚌 Buses 33 and 16 go to the centre of Joo Chiat, passing through Geylang; bus 14 goes from Orchard Rd to East Coast Rd. Bus 12 goes to East Coast Rd from Victoria St; bus 36 gets there from Bras Basah Rd.

Neighbourhood Map on p166

Koon Seng Road JOHN SEATON CALLAHAN/GETTY IMAGES ©

Walking Tour 🥾

Joo Chiat (Katong)

Also known as Katong, Joo Chiat is the heart of Singapore's Peranakan community. It's an evocative mix of multicoloured shophouses, tucked-away temples, and quaint workshops and studios – plus some of the city's best eating options. Try to head in during business hours, when locals hop in and out of heirloom shops in search of fabrics, produce and the next tasty snack.

Walk Facts

Start Geylang Serai Market (M Paya Lebar)

Finish Katong Antique House (🚌10, 12, 14, 32)

Length 2.5km; three to four hours

❶ Geylang Serai Market

Geylang Serai Market (1 Geylang Serai; ⏲8am-10pm) packs in a lively wet market, hawker food centre and stalls selling everything from Malay CDs to skull-caps. Feeling peckish? Hunt down some *pisang goreng* (banana fritters) and wash them down with *bandung* (milk with rose cordial syrup).

❷ Joo Chiat Road

Eclectic Joo Chiat Rd is lined with dusty antiques workshops, Islamic fashion boutiques and low-fuss grocery shops. Detour into Joo Chiat Tce to admire the Peranakan terraces at Nos 89 to 129, adorned with pintu pagar (swinging doors) and colourful ceramic tiles.

❸ Long Phung

Down-to-earth Vietnamese eatery **Long Phung** (☎9105 8519; 159 Joo Chiat Rd; dishes S\$7-23; ⏲noon-10pm) serves up some of Singapore's best Vietnamese food. The fragrant *pho* (noodle soup) and tangy mango salad are simply gorgeous.

❹ Kuan Im Tng Temple

Located on a quiet side street, Buddhist temple **Kuan Im Tng** (☎6348 0967; www.kuanimtng.org.sg; 62 Tembeling Rd, cnr Tembeling Rd & Joo Chiat Lane; admission free; ⏲5am-6pm) is dedicated to Kuan Yin, goddess of mercy. Temple fans will appreciate the ornate roof ridges adorned with dancing dragons.

❺ Koon Seng Road Terraces

Koon Seng Rd is famous for its two rows of pre-war, pastel-coloured Peranakan terrace houses (p167), lavished with stucco dragons, birds, crabs and brilliant glazed tiles imported from Europe.

❻ Sri Senpaga Vinayagar Temple

One of Singapore's most beautiful Hindu temples, **Sri Senpaga Vinayagar Temple** (☎6345 8176; www.senpaga.org.sg; 19 Ceylon Rd; admission free; ⏲6am-12.30pm & 5.30-11pm) features a *kamalapaatham*, a specially sculptured granite foot-stone found in certain ancient Hindu temples. The roof of the inner sanctum is covered in gold.

❼ Kim Choo Kueh Chang

Joo Chiat is stuffed with bakeries, but few equal old-school **Kim Choo Kueh Chang** (☎6741 2125; www.kimchoo.com; 109-111 East Coast Rd; ⏲9am-9pm). Pick up traditional pineapple tarts and other bite-sized Peranakan snacks, then pit stop at the adjoining boutique for Peranakan ceramics and clothing.

❽ Katong Antique House

Tiny shop-cum-museum **Katong Antique House** (☎6345 8544; 208 East Coast Rd; 45min tour S\$15; ⏲by appointment only, though it's sometimes open to the public) is the domain of Peter Wee, a noted expert on Peranakan culture, and packed with his collection of books, antiques and cultural artefacts.

A

Eunos Rd 2

B

Ⓜ Eunos

Sims Ave

Jln Eunos

C

D

⊗ N 0 _____ 500 m
0 _____ 0.25 miles

Changi Rd

1

Still Rd

For reviews see

⊙	Sights	p167
⊗	Eating	p168
⊖	Drinking	p170
⋆	Entertainment	p171
⊕	Shopping	p171

Jousting
Painters
Mural

Joo Chiat Tce

Telok Kurau Rd

Joo Chiat Rd

2

3 ⊙
11 ⊗

Joo Chiat Pl

**JOO CHIAT
(KATONG)**

Onan Rd

Tembeling Rd

⊗ 12

Joo Chiat La

4 ⊙

Crane Rd

Betel Box
The Real
Singapore
Tours

9 ⊗

Koon Seng Rd

Lorong L Teok Kurau

Still Rd

3

1 ⊙ Peranakan
Terrace
Houses

Dunman Rd

Duku Rd

Cheow Keng Rd

Tembeling Rd

East Coast Rd

13 ⊖

10 ⊗

Carpmael Rd

Joo Chiat Rd

Onan Rd

Ceylon Rd

St Patrick's Rd

Marshall Rd

Fowlie Rd

⊗ 8

Kuo Chuan Ave

Jago Cl

Chapel Rd

4

Haig Rd

6 ⊗ 7 ⊗ 15 ⊕
16 ⊕

East Coast Rd

17 ⊕

Joo Chiat Rd

Sea Ave

14 ⋆

Still Rd South

East Coast Rd

Brooke Rd

Parade Rd

5

Mountbatten Rd

Amber Gardens

Amber Rd

East Coast Rd

Marine Parade Rd

Roland
Restaurant

5 ⊙
Marine
Cove

Amber Rd

East Coast Pkwy (ECP)

East Coast
Park

⊙
2

6

East Coast Park Service Rd

*Strait of
Singapore*

A

B

C

D

Sights

Peranakan Terrace Houses

AREA

1 ◎ MAP P166, B3

Just off Joo Chiat Rd, Koon Seng Rd and Joo Chiat Pl feature Singapore's most extraordinary Peranakan terrace houses, joyously decorated with stucco dragons, birds, crabs and brilliantly glazed tiles. *Pintu pagar* (swinging doors) at the front of the houses are a typical feature, allowing cross breezes while retaining privacy. Those on Koon Seng Rd are located between Joo Chiat and Tembeling Rds, while those on Joo Chiat Pl run between Everitt and Mangis Rds. (Koon Seng Rd & Joo Chiat Pl; 🚌10, 14, 16, 32)

East Coast Park

PARK

2 ◎ MAP P166, C6

This 15km stretch of seafront park is where Singaporeans come to swim, windsurf, wakeboard, kayak, picnic, bicycle, rollerblade, skateboard, and – of course – eat. You'll find swaying coconut palms, patches of bushland, a lagoon, sea-sports clubs and some excellent eating options.Renting a bike, enjoying the sea breezes, watching the veritable city of container ships out in the strait and capping it all off with a beachfront meal is one of the most pleasant ways to spend a Singapore afternoon. (📞1800 471 7300; www.nparks.gov.sg; 🅿; 🚌36, 43, 48, 196, 197, 401)

Jousting Painters Mural

PUBLIC ART

3 ◎ MAP P166, A2

This giant mural by Lithuanian-born street artist Ernest Zacharevic (www.ernestzacharevic.com) is fantastically playful, like all his works. It features two very real-looking boys prepared for battle on brightly painted horses. (cnr Everitt Rd & Joo Chiat Tce; Ⓜ Paya Lebar)

Betel Box: The Real Singapore Tours

TOURS

4 ◎ MAP P166, A2

Insider tours led by Tony Tan and the team at Betel Box Hostel. Choose from culture and heritage walks, city kick scootering or food odysseys through the historic Joo Chiat, Kampong Glam or Chinatown neighbourhoods. If you're looking for a walk on the wild side, join the Friday night tour through red-light district in Geylang. (📞6247 7340; www.betelboxtours.com; 200 Joo Chiat Rd; S$60-100; tours Ⓜ Paya Lebar)

Marine Cove

PARK

5 ◎ MAP P166, D5

With a breezy seaside setting, this 3,500-sq-metre playground is the perfect place to let the kids run wild. Highlights include an 8m tall lighthouse gym, rock-climbing walls and digital game stations. A row of family-friendly restaurants complete this kiddie enclave. Weekday afternoons are the best times to go (weekends are manic), and don't forget your hat as there's little shade. (📞1800 471 7300; www.nparks.gov.sg; 1000 East Coast Park; admission free; ⊙24hr; P 🚻; 🚌36, 43, 48, 196, 197, 401)

Eating

328 Katong Laksa   MALAYSIAN $

6 ❌ MAP P166, B4

For a bargain foodie high, hit this cult-status corner shop. The star is the namesake laksa: thin rice noodles in a light curry broth made with coconut milk and coriander, and topped with shrimps and cockles. Order a side of *otah* (spiced mackerel cake grilled in a banana leaf) and wash it down with a cooling glass of lime juice.

(📞9732 8163; www.328katonglaksa.com; 51 East Coast Rd; laksa S$5.50-7.50; ⊙10am-10pm; 🚌10, 12, 14, 32)

Birds of Paradise   GELATO $

7 ❌ MAP P166, B4

This high-end boutique ice-cream shop is stocked with artisanal gelatos, taking flavour cues from nature: think white chrysanthemum and strawberry basil. Even the cone (S$1 extra) gets the botanical touch, infused with a subtle thyme fragrance. In homage to Singapore's heritage, there are also local flavours – try the heady masala spice, if available. (📞9678 6092; www.facebook.com/bopgelato; 01-05, 63 East Coast Rd; ⊙noon-10pm Tue-Sun; 🚌10, 14, 16, 32)

Katong laksa (spicy coconut broth with noodles)

LIONEL NG/GETTY IMAGES ©

The Invention of Chilli Crab

In 1956, Mr and Mrs Lim opened a seafood restaurant called the Palm Beach. It was here that Mrs Lim first concocted the now-famous tomato, chilli and egg sauce that makes the quintessential Singapore chilli crab. At least that's the story according to her son, who decades, on is the proprietor of his own giant restaurant, **Roland Restaurant** (Map p166, C5; 6440 8205; www.rolandrestaurant.com.sg; 06-750 Block 89, Marine Parade Central, Deck J, multistorey carpark; dishes S$12-60, crab per kg from S$73; 11.30am-2.15pm & 6-10.15pm; 36, 48, 196, 197), where the chilli crab lures former prime minister Goh Chok Tong on National Day. The crabs are fleshy and sweet and the gravy milder than many of its competitors: good news if you're not a big spice fan.

Chin Mee Chin Confectionery
BAKERY $

8 MAP P166, C4

A nostalgia trip for many older Singaporeans, old-style bakeries such as Chin Mee Chin are a dying breed, with their geometric floors, wooden chairs and industrious aunties pouring *kopi* (coffee). One of the few Singaporean breakfast joints that still makes its own *kaya* (coconut jam), it's also a good spot to pick up some pastries to go. (6345 0419; 204 East Coast Rd; kaya toast & coffee from S$2; 8.30am-3.30pm Tue-Sun; 10, 12, 14, 32)

Loving Hut
VEGAN $$

9 MAP P166, A3

Bright, airy and oozing healthy vibes, this strictly plant-based cafe serves up traditional local fare. Try the sesame chicken clay-pot rice or manbo fillet with chilli nyonya mee siam; all are 100% vegan. (6348 6318; www.loving hut.com.sg; 01-01, 229 Joo Chiat Rd; dishes S$8-20; 11.30am-2.30pm & 6-9pm Mon, Wed-Fri, 11.30am-9pm Sat & Sun; 10, 14, 16, 32)

Penny University
CAFE $

10 MAP P166, D3

Coffee snobs will appreciate this laid-back new-schooler, one of the few speciality coffeeshops on the East Coast. Grab a booth or sit at the communal table, sip an espresso and scan the menu for fresh, modern grub such as vanilla-infused yoghurt with granola or Turkish eggs (poached, on whipped yoghurt, topped with spicy Moroccan harissa sauce and oregano). (6345 9055; www.face book.com/pennyuniversity; 402 East Coast Rd; dishes S$6-16; 8.30am-6pm, to 10.30pm Fri & Sat, to 7pm Sun; 10, 12, 14, 32)

Nonya Desserts

Peranakan (Nonya) desserts are typified by *kueh* (colourful rice cakes often flavoured with coconut and palm sugar) and sweet, sticky delicacies such as miniature pineapple tarts that are sold everywhere in small plastic tubs with red lids. The magnificent *kueh lapis,* a laborious layer cake, is a must-try. Head to old-school Kim Choo Kueh Chang (p165) to sample some of the island's best.

Smokey's BBQ
AMERICAN $$

11 ⓧ MAP P166, A2

You'll be longing for sweet home Alabama at this breezy, all-American barbecue legend. Californian owner Rob makes all the dry rubs using secret recipes and the meats are smoked using hickory and mesquite woodchips straight from the USA. Start with the spicy buffalo wings with blue-cheese dipping sauce, then stick to slow-roasted, smoked meats such as ridiculously tender, fall-off-the-bone ribs. (☎ 6345 6914; www.smokeysbbq.com.sg; 73 Joo Chiat Pl; mains S$19-65; ☻3-11pm, from 11am Sat & Sun; 🛜; Ⓜ Paya Lebar)

Guan Hoe Soon
PERANAKAN $$

12 ⓧ MAP P166, A2

Famously, this is Singapore's oldest Peranakan restaurant (established 1953) and the late former-prime minister Lee Kuan Yew's favourite ... but even boasts like that don't cut much ice with picky Singaporeans if the food doesn't match up. Fortunately, its fame hasn't inspired complacency and the Nonya food here is top-notch. The definitive Peranakan *ayam buah keluak* (chicken in black nut) is a standout. (☎ 6344 2761; www.guanhoesoon.com; 38 Joo Chiat Pl; mains S$11-16; ☻11am-3pm & 6-9.30pm; Ⓜ Paya Lebar)

Drinking

Cider Pit
BAR

13 ⓖ MAP P166, B3

Wedged in a nondescript concrete structure, Cider Pit is easy to miss. Don't. The watering hole offers an extensive range of ciders on tap, and speciality beers such as Australia's Little Creatures. It's a refreshingly casual, unfussy kind of place, ideal for easygoing drinking sessions among expats in shorts, tees and flip-flops. (☎ 6440 0504; www.eastofavalon wines.com; 328 Joo Chiat Rd; ☻3pm-1am, from 1pm Sat & Sun; 🛜; Ⓜ Paya Lebar)

Entertainment

Necessary Stage
THEATRE

⭐ 14 ⭐ MAP P166, D4

Since the theatre's inception in 1987, artistic director Alvin Tan has collaborated with resident playwright Haresh Sharma to produce over 60 original works. Innovative, indigenous and often controversial, the Necessary Stage is one of Singapore's best-known theatre groups. Productions are performed at the Necessary Stage Black Box and other venues; check the website for current shows and purchase tickets through SISTIC (p49). (☎ 6440 8115; www.necessary.org; B1-02 Marine Parade Community Bldg, 278 Marine Parade Rd; 🚍 12, 16, 36, 196)

Shopping

Rumah Bebe
CLOTHING, HANDICRAFTS

🔒 15 🔒 MAP P166, B4

Bebe Seet is the owner of this 1928 shophouse and purveyor of all things Peranakan. She sells traditional kebayas (Nonya-style blouses with decorative lace) with contemporary twists and beautifully beaded shoes. If you've got time and the inclination, you can take one of the beading classes run by Bebe, including a two-session beginners course (S$450). (☎ 6247 8781; www.rumahbebe.com; 113 East Coast Rd; ⏰ 9.30am-6.30pm Tue-Sun; 🚍 10, 14, 16, 32)

Rumah Bebe

JASON KNOTT/ALAMY ©

Peranakan Culture

Peranakan heritage has been enjoying renewed interest, mainly triggered by *The Little Nonya,* a high-rating 2008 drama series focused on a Peranakan family, and the opening of Singapore's outstanding Peranakan Museum (p46). But who are the Peranakans?

Origins

In Singapore, Peranakan (locally born) people are the descendants of immigrants who married local, mostly Malay women. The largest Peranakan group in Singapore is the Straits Chinese. The men, called Babas, and the women, Nonya, primarily speak a patois that mixes Bahasa Malaysia, Hokkien dialect and English. The ancestors of the Straits Chinese were mainly traders from mainland China, their presence on the Malay peninsula stretching back to the Ming dynasty. The ancestors of Chitty Melaka and Jawi Peranakan were Indian traders, whose unions with local Malay women created their own unique traditions. All three groups are defined by an intriguing, hybrid culture created by centuries of cultural exchange and adaptation.

Weddings

No Peranakan tradition matches the scale of the traditional wedding. Originally spanning 12 days, its fusion of Fujian Chinese and Malay traditions included the consulting of a *sinseh pokwa* (astrologer) in the choosing of an auspicious wedding day, elaborate gifts delivered to the bride's parents in *bakul siah* (lacquered bamboo containers) and a young boy rolling across the bed three times in the hope for a male first-born. With the groom in Qing-dynasty scholar garb and the bride in a similarly embroidered gown and hat piece, the first day would include a tea ceremony. On the second day, the couple took their first meal together, feeding each other 12 dishes to symbolise the 12-day process, while the third day would see them offering tea to their parents and in-laws. On the *dua belah hari* (12th-day ceremony), the marriage was sealed and proof of the consummation confirmed with a discreet sighting of the stain on the bride's virginity handkerchief by the bride's parents and groom's mother.

Cat Socrates GIFTS & SOUVENIRS

16 🔒 MAP P166, B4

Complete with feline 'assistant shopkeeper', this eclectic boutique is filled with wares from independent local and foreign designers. Creatives flock here for the mix of whimsical stationery, lo-fi cameras, on-trend homewares, stylish jewellery and indie books. Souvenir hunters will love the Singapore–inspired curios, especially the Peranakan-themed notebooks and tiles. (📞6348 0863; https://cat-socrates.myshopify.com; 448 Joo Chiat Rd; ⏰12.30-9.30pm Tue-Sun; 🚌10, 14, 16, 32)

112 Katong MALL

17 🔒 MAP P166, B4

This contemporary mall is where East Coasters love to shop. You will find plenty of fashion and lifestyle stores, as well as a large outlet of design-lover's favourite, **Naiise** (www.naiise.com), known for its fun Singaporean trinkets and trendy homewares.

Kids will love the water playground on the 4th floor. (📞6636 2112; www.112katong.com.sg; 112 East Coast Rd; ⏰10am-10pm; 🚌10, 14, 16, 32)

Worth a Trip 🥾

Pulau Ubin

Singapore's 'Far East' has a slower, nostalgic style of local life. Vests, boardshorts and flip-flops are the look in chilled-out Changi Village, a place where low-rise buildings are the norm and out-of-towners are a less common sight. A short bumboat (motorised sampan) ride away, the rustic island of Pulau Ubin is the Singapore that development has left behind … for now.

Getting There

Ⓜ Catch the East–West Line to Tanah Merah MRT Station.

🚌 Take bus 2 to Changi Village.

⛴ For Pulau Ubin catch a bumboat from Changi Point Ferry Terminal.

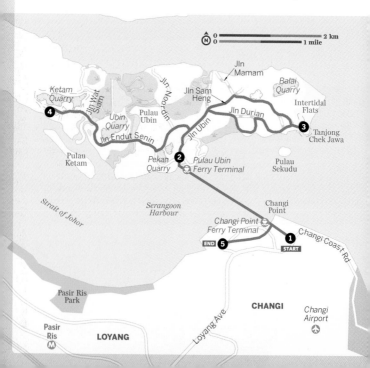

❶ Changi Village

Hugging Singapore's far north-east coast, Changi Village is well worth a wander to experience a curiously relaxed side of Singapore. The vibe is almost village-like, and a browse around the area will turn up cheap clothes, batik, Indian textiles and electronics. Bumboats to Pulau Ubin depart from Changi Point Ferry Terminal (p180), beside the bus terminal.

❷ Pulau Ubin Village

Your landing spot on Pulau Ubin is Pulau Ubin Village. Although not technically a tourist sight, its ramshackle nature channels a long-lost Singapore. If you're feeling peckish, turn left for a handful of places to eat, mostly housed in *kampong* (village) huts. The village is also the place to rent bikes; day rentals cost around S$6 to S$25.

❸ Chek Jawa Wetlands

If you only have time for one part of Pulau Ubin, make it **Chek Jawa Wetlands** (☎1800 471 7300; www.nparks.gov.sg; admission free; ◷8.30am-6pm). Located at the island's eastern end, its 1km coastal boardwalk juts out into the sea before looping back through protected mangrove swamp to the 20m-high Jejawi Tower, offering a stunning panorama.

❹ German Girl Shrine

The German Girl Shrine, near Ketam Quarry, is one of the island's quirkier sights. Legend has it that the young German daughter of a coffee-plantation manager was running away from British troops who had come to arrest her parents during WWI and fell fatally into a quarry. Somewhere along the way, this daughter of a Roman Catholic family became a Taoist deity.

❺ Coastal Settlement

Back in Changi, end the day with drinks at **Coastal Settlement** (☎6475 0200; www.thecoastal settlement.com; 200 Netheravon Rd; ◷10.30am-11pm Tue-Thu, to midnight Fri, from 8.30am Sat & Sun; 🛜), an eclectic bar-lounge-restaurant pimped with retro objects and set in a black-and-white colonial bungalow on lush, verdant grounds.

Survival Guide

Singapore skyline SAKDAWUT TANGTONGSAP/SHUTTERSTOCK ©

Before You Go

Book Your Stay

Staying in Singapore is expensive, especially in the CBD and around shoppers paradise Orchard Rd. However more modest and budget-friendly digs are available in the surrounding areas of Little India and Chinatown. Prices all over the island skyrocket during September's F1 night race so you should book early if visiting at that time. Accommodation options range from simple, shared back-packer dorms to some of the most historical and luxurious sleep spots in Asia.

Useful Websites

Lonely Planet (lonelyplanet.com/singapore/hotels) Recommendations and bookings.

StayinSingapore (www.stayinsingapore.com) Hotel-booking website managed by the Singapore Hotel Association.

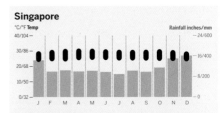

Singapore

°C/°F Temp

Rainfall inches/mm

When to Go

○ **Jan & Feb** Buzzing night markets and Chinese New Year celebrations.

○ **Jun & Jul** School holidays fall in June and July, the hottest time of year, so try to avoid travelling in these months if possible.

○ **Dec** Moonsoon rains cool Singapore down a fraction.

LateRooms (www.laterooms.com) Great deals on rooms; book now and pay when you stay.

Best Budget

Adler Hostel (www.adlerhostel.com) This self-proclaimed 'poshtel' just near the Chinatown MRT comes with Chinese antiques.

COO (www.staycoo.com) A new-school hostel with neon lighting and a hip location in Tiong Bahru.

Dream Lodge (www.dreamlodge.sg) Spick-and-span capsule hostel in up-and-coming Jalan Besar.

BEAT. Capsules (www.beathostel.co) Sleek capsules smack bang on the Singapore River.

Kam Leng Hotel (www.kamleng.com) Retro hotel in the Jalan Besar district.

Best Midrange

Wanderlust (www.wanderlusthotel.com) Idiosyncratic rooms packed with imagination and designer twists in intriguing Little India.

Lloyd's Inn (www.lloydsinn.com) Minimalist boutique hotel a short stroll from Orchard Rd.

Holiday Inn Express Orchard Road (www.hiexpress.com) A fresh, good-value option just a block from Orchard Rd.

Hotel Indigo (www.hotelindigo.com) Peranakan-inspired hotel bursting with nostalgic memorabilia, steps from heritage-heavy Joo Chiat Rd.

Great Madras (www.thegreatmadras.com) Pastel art-deco gem right in the thick of Little India.

Best Top End

Fullerton Bay Hotel (www.fullertonhotels.com) Elegant, light-filled luxury perched right on Marina Bay.

Parkroyal on Pickering (www.parkroyalhotels.com) A striking architectural statement, with hanging gardens and a stunning infinity pool.

Capella Singapore (www.capellahotels.com) Cascading pools, lush gardens and chic interiors on Sentosa.

Six Senses Duxton (www.sixsenses.com) A tranquil haven, where no two rooms are the same, ensconced in a row of heritage shophouses.

Warehouse (www.thewarehousehotel.com) Industrial-chic interiors and a stunning infinity pool right by the Singapore River.

Arriving in Singapore

By Plane

Changi Airport (📞 6595 6868; www.changiairport.com; Airport Blvd; 📶; Ⓜ Changi Airport), 20km northeast of Singapore's central business district (CBD), has four main terminals with a fifth in the works. Regularly voted the world's best airport, it is a major international gateway, with frequent flights to all corners of the globe. You'll find free internet, courtesy phones for local calls, foreign-exchange booths, medical centres, left luggage, hotels, day spas, showers, a gym, a swimming pool and no shortage of shops.

The much-anticipated Jewel Changi Airport is a 10-storey complex with exciting attractions, including a canopy park, forest and rain vortex as well as retail, accommodation and dining offerings. At the time of research, it was slated to open in early 2019.

Transport options from Changi Airport include the following:

○ MRT trains run into town from the airport from 5.30am to 11.18pm; public buses run from 6am to midnight. The train and bus trips cost from S$1.69.

○ The airport shuttle bus (adult/child S$9/6) runs into the city 24 hours a day.

○ A taxi into the city will cost anywhere from S$20 to S$40, and up to 50% more between midnight and 6am, plus airport surcharges.

○ A four-seater limousine taxi from the airport to the city is S$55, plus S$15 surcharge per additional stop.

By Bus

Numerous private companies run comfortable bus services to Singapore from many destinations in Malaysia, including Melaka and Kuala Lumpur, as well as from cities such as Hat Yai in Thailand. Many of these services terminate at **Golden Mile Complex Bus Terminal** (5001 Beach Rd; Ⓜ Bugis, Nicoll Hwy), near Kampong Glam. You can book at www. busonlineticket.com.

From Johor Bahru, commuter buses with Causeway Link Express (www.cause waylink.com.my) run regularly to various locations in Singapore (one way S$3.50/ RM3.40, every 15 to 30 minutes, roughly 6am to 11.30pm), including Newton Circus, Jurong East Bus Terminal and Kranji MRT station.

By Train

Malaysian company Keretapi Tanah Melayu Berhad (www. ktmb.com.my) runs trains from Kuala Lumpur to JB Sentral station in Johor Bahru from where you get a shuttle train to **Woodlands Train Checkpoint** (11 Woodlands Crossing; 🚌 170, Causeway Link Express from Queen St terminal). Tickets for the shuttle (S$5) can be bought at the

counter. Trains leave from here to Kuala Lumpur, with connections on to Thailand. You can book tickets at the Woodlands or JB Sentral stations or online at www. easybook.com.

By Ferry

Ferry services from Malaysia and Indonesia arrive at various ferry terminals in Singapore.
Changi Point Ferry Terminal (📞 6545 2305; 51 Lorong Bekukong; 🕐 24hr; 🚌 2)

HarbourFront Cruise & Ferry Terminal (📞 6513 2200; www.sing aporecruise.com; 1 Maritime Sq; 📶 ; Ⓜ HarbourFront)

Tanah Merah Ferry Terminal (📞 6513 2200; www.singaporecruise.com. sg; 50 Tanah Merah Ferry Rd; 🚌 35)

Getting Around

Mass Rapid Transit (MRT)

The efficient Mass Rapid Transit (MRT) subway system is the

easiest, quickest and most comfortable way to get around Singapore. The system operates from 5.30am to midnight, with trains at peak times running every two to three minutes, and every five to seven minutes off-peak.

The system consists of five colour-coded lines: North–South (red), North–East (purple), East–West (green), Circle Line (orange) and Downtown (blue). A sixth line, the Thomson–East Coast Line (brown), will open in five stages, with the first scheduled to open in 2019.

Single-trip tickets cost from S$1.40 to S$2.50, but if you're using the MRT a lot it can become a hassle buying tickets for every journey. A lot more convenient is the EZ-Link card (www.ezlink. com.sg). Alternatively, a **Singapore Tourist Pass** (www.thesing aporetouristpass. com.sg) offers unlimited train and bus travel (S$10 plus a S$10 refundable deposit) for one day.

Bus

Singapore's extensive bus service is clean, efficient and regular, reaching every corner of the island. The two main operators are **SBS Transit** (📞1800 225 5663; www.sbstransit.com.sg) and **SMRT** (📞1800 336 8900; www.smrt.com.sg). Both offer similar services.

Bus fares range from S$1 to S$2.10 (less with an EZ-Link card). When you board the bus, drop the exact money into the fare box (no change is given), or tap your EZ-Link card or Singapore Tourist Pass on the reader as you board, then again when you get off.

Train operator SMRT also runs late-night bus services between the city and various suburbs from 11.30pm to 4.35am on Fridays, Saturdays and the eve of public holidays. The flat rate per journey is S$4.50. See the website for route details.

Taxi

You can flag down a taxi any time, but in the city centre taxis are technically not allowed to stop anywhere except at designated taxi stands.

Finding a taxi in the city at certain times is harder than it should be. These include during peak hours, at night, or when it's raining. Many cab drivers change shifts between 4pm and 5pm, making it notoriously difficult to score a taxi then.

The fare system is also complicated, but thankfully it's all metered, so there's no haggling over fares. The basic flagfall is S$3 to S$3.40 then S$0.22 for every 400m.

There's a whole raft of surcharges to note, among them 50% of the metered fare from midnight to 6am and 25% of the metered fare between 6am and 9.30am Monday to Friday, and 6pm to midnight daily. Airport journeys incur a surcharge of S$5 from 5pm to midnight Friday to Sunday and S$3 at all other times. There's also a S$3 city-area surcharge from 5pm to midnight and S$2.30 to S$8 for telephone bookings.

Tipping is not generally expected, but it's courteous to round up or tell the driver to keep the change.

Payment by credit card incurs a 10% surcharge. You can also pay using your EZ-Link transport card. For a comprehensive list of fares and surcharges, visit www.taxising apore.com.

Comfort Taxi & City Cab (📞6552 1111; www.cdgtaxi.com.sg)

Premier Taxis (📞6363 6888; www.premiertaxi.com.sg)

SMRT Taxis (📞6555 8888; www.smrt.com.sg)

Essential Information

Accessible Travel

A wide-ranging and long-term government campaign has seen ramps, lifts and other facilities progressively installed around the island. Footpaths in the city are nearly all immaculate. MRT station all have lifts and more than half of public buses are wheelchair-friendly. Wheelchair-accessible taxis can sometimes be flagged down, but contact **SGMAXI.cab** (www.sgmaxi.cab) to book wheelchair-accessible maxicabs for airport transfers or transport around the island.

The **Disabled People's Association Singapore** (www.dpa.org.sg) can provide information on accessibility in Singapore.

Download Lonely Planet's free Accessible Travel guides (http://lptravel.to/AccessibleTravel).

Business Hours

Banks 9.30am to 4.30pm Monday to Friday (some till 6pm or later); 9.30am to noon or later Saturday.

Restaurants Generally noon to 2.30pm and 6pm to 11pm. Casual restaurants and food courts open all day.

Shops 10am or 11am to 6pm; larger shops and department stores til 9.30pm or 10pm. Some smaller shops in Chinatown and Arab St close on Sundays.

Discount Cards

If you arrived on a Singapore Airlines or SilkAir flight, you can get discounts at shops, restaurants and attractions by presenting your boarding pass. See www.singaporeair.com/boardingpass for information.

Electricity

Type G
230V/50Hz

Emergencies

Country Code	65
Ambulance & Fire	995
Police	999

LGBT+ Travellers

Sex between males is illegal in Singapore and carries a minimum sentence of 10 years. Singaporeans are fairly conservative about public affection.

Despite that, Singapore has a string of popular LGBT+ bars. Websites **Travel Gay Asia** (www.travelgayasia.com), **PLUguide** (www.pluguide.com) or **Utopia** (www.utopia-asia.com) have coverage of venues and events.

Money

ATMs and money-changers are widely available. Credit cards are accepted in most shops and restaurants.

Currency

The country's unit of currency is the Singapore dollar (S$), locally referred to as the 'sing dollar', which is made up of 100 cents. Singapore uses 5¢, 10¢, 20¢, 50¢ and S$1 coins, while notes come in denominations of S$2, S$5, S$10, S$50, S$100, S$500 and S$1000.

Credit Cards

Credit cards are widely accepted, apart from at local hawkers and food courts.

Public Holidays

The only holiday that has a major effect on the city is Chinese New Year, when virtually all shops shut down for two days. Public holidays are as follows:

New Year's Day 1 January

Chinese New Year Two days in January/February

Good Friday March/April

Labour Day 1 May

Vesak Day May

Hari Raya Puasa June

National Day 9 August

Hari Raya Haji August

Dewali October

Christmas Day 25 December

Taxes & Refunds

Visitors can get a refund of the 7% GST on purchases, under the following conditions:

○ Present your passport and spend a minimum of S$100 at one retailer on the same day, for no more than three purchases.

○ Get an eTRS (Electronic Tourist Refund Scheme) ticket issued by the shop or use a debit or credit card as a token to track purchases; no need to pay with the card.

○ Scan your eTRS ticket or token debit/credit card at the self-help kiosks at the airport or cruise terminal. If physical inspection of the goods is required present the goods, original receipts and your boarding pass at the Customs Inspection Counter.

Tourist Information

Singapore Visitors Centre @ Orchard (Map p84, F5; ☏ 1800 736 2000; www.yoursingapore.com; 216 Orchard Rd; ◷ 8.30am-9.30pm; ☏; Ⓜ Somerset) This main branch is filled with knowledgable staff who can help you organise tours, buy tickets and book hotels.

Visas

Citizens of most countries are granted 90-day entry on arrival. Citizens of India, the People's Republic of China, the Commonwealth of Independent States and most Middle Eastern countries must obtain a visa before arriving. Visa extensions can be applied for at the **Immigration & Checkpoints Authority** website (☏ 6391 6100; www.ica.gov.sg; Level 4, ICA Bldg, 10 Kallang Rd; ◷ 8am-4pm Mon-Fri; Ⓜ Lavender).

Customs Regulations

You are not allowed to bring tobacco into Singapore unless you pay duty. You will be slapped with a hefty fine if you fail to declare and pay. You are permitted 1L each of wine, beer and spirits duty-free. Alternatively, you are allowed 2L of wine and 1L of beer, or 2L of beer and 1L of wine. You need to have been out of Singapore for more than 48 hours and to anywhere but Malaysia. It's illegal to bring chewing gum, firecrackers, obscene or seditious material, gun-shaped cigarette lighters, endangered species or their by-products, and pirated recordings or publications with you.

Language

The official languages of Singapore are Malay, Mandarin, Tamil and English. Malay is the national language, adopted when Singapore was part of Malaysia, but its use is mostly restricted to the Malay community.

The government's long-standing campaign to promote Mandarin, the main nondialectal Chinese language, has been very successful and increasing numbers of Singaporean Chinese speak it at home. In this chapter we've provided Pinyin (the official system of writing Mandarin in the Roman alphabet) alongside the Mandarin script.

Tamil is the main Indian language in Singapore; others include Malayalam and Hindi. If you read our pronunciation guides for the Tamil phrases in this chapter as if they were English, you'll be understood. The stressed syllables are indicated with italics.

English is widespread and has been the official first language of instruction in schools since 1987. Travellers will have no trouble getting by with only English in Singapore.

To enhance your trip with a phrasebook, visit lonelyplanet.com. Lonely Planet iPhone phrasebooks are available through the Apple App store.

Malay

Hello. — Helo.

Goodbye. (when leaving/staying) — Selamat tinggal./ Selamat jalan.

How are you? — Apa khabar?

Fine, thanks. — Khabar baik.

Please. (when asking/offering) — Tolong./ Silakan.

Thank you. — Terima kasih.

Excuse me. — Maaf.

Sorry. — Minta maaf.

Yes./No. — Ya./Tidak.

What's your name — Siapa nama kamu?

My name is ... — Nama saya ...

Do you speak English? — Bolehkah anda berbicara Bahasa Inggeris?

I don't understand. — Saya tidak faham.

How much is it? — Berapa harganya?

Can I see the menu? — Minta senarai makanan?

Please bring the bill. — Tolong bawa bil.

Where are the toilets? — Tandas di mana?

Help! — Tolong!

Mandarin

Hello./Goodbye.
你好。/再见。好。你呢？ — Nǐhǎo./ Zàijiàn. Hǎo. Nǐ ne?

How are you?
你好吗？ — Nǐhǎo ma?

Fine. And you?
好。你呢？ — Hǎo. Nǐ ne?

Please ...
请…… — Qǐng ...

Thank you.
谢谢你。 — Xièxie nǐ.

Excuse me. (to get attention)
劳驾。   *Láojià.*

Excuse me. (to get past)
借光。   *Jièguāng.*

Sorry.
对不起。   *Duìbùqǐ.*

Yes./No.
是。/不是。   *Shì./Bùshì.*

What's your name?
你叫什么   *Nǐ jiào shénme*
名字?   *míngzi?*

My name is ...
我叫……   *Wǒ jiào ...*

Do you speak English?
你会说   *Nǐ huìshuō*
英文吗?   *Yīngwén ma?*

I don't understand.
我不明白。   *Wǒ bù míngbái.*

How much is it?
多少钱?   *Duōshǎo qián?*

Can I see the menu?
能不能给我看   *Néng bù néng gěiwǒ*
一下菜单?   *kàngyīxià càidān?*

Please bring the bill.
请给我账单。   *Qǐng gěiwǒ*
zhàngdān.

Where are the toilets?
厕所在哪儿?   *Cèsuǒ zài nǎr?*

Help!
救命!   *Jiùmìng!*

Tamil

Hello.
வணக்கம்.   *va·nak·kam*

Goodbye.
போய வருகிறேன்.   *po·i va·ru·ki·reyn*

How are you?
நீங்கள் நலமா?   *neeng·kal na·la·maa*

Fine, thanks. And you?
நலம், நன்றி.   *na·lam nan·dri*
நீங்கள்?   *neeng·kal?*

Please.
தயவு செய்து.   *ta·ya·vu chey·tu*

Thank you.
நன்றி.   *nan·dri*

Excuse me.
தயவு செய்து.   *ta·ya·vu sei·du*

Sorry.
மன்னிக்கவும்.   *man·nik·ka·vum*

Yes./No.
ஆமாம். / இல்லை.   *aa·maam/il·lai*

What's your name?
உங்கள் பெயர்   *ung·kal pe·yar*
என்ன?   *en·na*

My name is ...
என் பெயர்...   *en pe·yar ...*

Do you speak English?
நீங்கள் ஆங்கிலம்   *neeng·kal*
பேசுவீர்களா?   *aang·ki·lam*
    pey·chu·veer·ka·la

I don't understand.
எனக்கு   *e·nak·ku*
விளங்கவில்லை.   *vi·lang·ka·vil·lai*

How much is it?
இது என்ன   *i·tu en·na*
விலை?   *vi·lai*

I'd like the bill/menu, please.
எனக்கு தயவு   *e·nak·ku ta·ya·vu*
செய்து   *chey·tu*
விலைச்சீட்டு/   *vi·laich·cheet·tu/*
உணவுப்பட்டியல்   *u·na·vup·pat·ti·yal*
கொடுங்கள்.   *ko·tung·kal*

Where are the toilets?
கழிவறைகள்   *ka·zi·va·rai·kal*
எங்கே?   *eng·key*

Help!
உதவி!   *u·ta·vi*

Behind the Scenes

Send Us Your Feedback

We love to hear from travellers – your comments help make our books better. We read every word, and we guarantee that your feedback goes straight to the authors. Visit **lonelyplanet.com/contact** to submit your updates and suggestions.

Note: We may edit, reproduce and incorporate your comments in Lonely Planet products such as guidebooks, websites and digital products, so let us know if you don't want your comments reproduced or your name acknowledged. For a copy of our privacy policy visit lonelyplanet.com/privacy.

Ria's Thanks

Thank you to my Destination Editor Tanya Parker for all her help in guiding me through my Lonely Planet adventure, and to all those I met along my travels who kindly shared their knowledge, time and Singapore secrets with me. To Craig, Cisca and William, my travelling circus tribe.

Acknowledgements

Cover photograph: OCBC Skyway, The Supertree Grove, Gardens by the Bay, Singapore, John Harper/ Getty Images ©

Photographs pp 30-31 (clockwise from left):
siraphat/SHUTTERSTOCK ©,
Komar/SHUTTERSTOCK ©,
tapanuth/SHUTTERSTOCK ©,
Peter Adams/Getty Images ©,
leungchopan/Getty Images ©

This 6th edition of Lonely Planet's *Pocket Singapore* guidebook was researched and written by Ria de Jong. The previous two editions were written by Ria and Cristian Bonetto. This guidebook was produced by the following:

Destination Editor
Tanya Parker

Senior Product Editor
Kate Chapman

Regional Senior Cartographer
Julie Sheridan

Product Editor
Claire Rourke

Book Designer
Fergal Condon

Assisting Editors
Judith Bamber, Sandie Kestell, Rosie Nicholson, Jessica Ryan, Gabrielle Stefanos, Angela Tinson, Monica Woods

Assisting Cartographer
Mark Griffiths

Cover Researcher
Wibowo Rusli

Thanks to:
Ronan Abayawickrema, Gwen Cotter, Marcus Feaver, Martin Heng, Amy Lynch, Kate Morgan, Claire Naylor, Karyn Noble, Genna Patterson, Eleanor Simpson, James Smart, Peter Tudor

Index

See also separate subindexes for:

⊗ **Eating p189**

⊖ **Drinking p190**

✪ **Entertainment p191**

🔒 **Shopping p191**

Sights 000
Map Pages 000

Our Writer

Ria de Jong

Ria started life in Asia, born in Sri Lanka to Dutch/Australian parents. She has always relished the hustle and excitement of this continent of contrasts. After growing up in Townsville, Australia, Ria moved to Sydney as a features writer before packing her bags for a five-year stint in the Philippines. Moving to Singapore in 2015 with her husband and two small children, Ria is loving discovering every nook and cranny of this tiny city, country, nation. This is Ria's third Singapore update for Lonely Planet. Follow Ria on Twitter @ria_in_transit.

Published by Lonely Planet Global Limited
CRN 554153
6th edition – June 2019
ISBN 978 1 78657 843 3
© Lonely Planet 2019   Photographs © as indicated 2019
10 9 8 7 6 5 4 3 2 1
Printed in Malaysia